Five Anti-Catholic Myths

Slavery, Crusades, Inquisition, Galileo, Holocaust

✝

Gerard M. Verschuuren

Five Anti-Catholic Myths

Slavery
Crusades
Inquisition
Galileo
Holocaust

Angelico Press

First published
by Angelico Press 2015
© Gerard M. Verschuuren 2015

For information, address:
Angelico Press
4709 Briar Knoll Dr.
Kettering, OH 45429
angelicopress.com

978-1-62138-128-0 (pbk)
978-1-62138-129-7 (ebook)

Cover design: Michael Schrauzer

CONTENTS

Preface

The myths we are going to analyze in this book claim to lay bare the "dirty history" of the Catholic Church. These are myths fabricated by people with a strong bias against the Catholic Church. They are based more on fiction than on non-fiction. They distort the facts. Catholics seem to be a perfect target for these kinds of attacks—partially because they tend to remain silent in the face of cultures that are largely hostile to all things Catholic.

The Catholic Church's "dirty history" is not that dirty at all. As Pope Leo XIII once said, the Catholic Church has no reason to fear historical truth. Yet some Catholics as well as many non-Catholics often see history through a lens that has been shaped by post-Reformation propaganda or by 18th century Enlightenment prejudices. Just as these myths served a purpose in the Reformation and were perpetuated in the 18th century Enlightenment and the 19th century world of progress and scientism, they still serve a purpose in today's secularist climate. Does that really validate them?

In my writing, I "borrowed" much valuable material from others. This is not a scholarly work—although it is based on scholarly work—so I decided, in order to keep the book accessible to the more general reader, not to use footnotes with more detailed references to sources I used. Nowadays, most people are able to check the reliability of my claims on the Internet anyway, all by themselves. But I do warn you that many sources out there use a "revisionist" version of history, often colored by the myths I am trying to debunk in this book.

At the end of the book (see Suggested Reading), I suggest a small selection of some good sources for further information, which were also very helpful to me, most especially Roy Schoeman's masterpiece, *Salvation is from the Jews*.

Myth 1
Slavery under a Catholic Veil

I don't think anyone would dare to proclaim that slavery is a Christian or Catholic invention. That, as we will see shortly, would be too obvious a distortion of the facts. But there are still people who argue that Christianity, and the Catholic Church in particular, kept slavery in existence and helped it even spread around the world by slave trade and colonialism. They grill the Catholic Church: was she not founded by Jesus Christ, the Son of God, to proclaim and uphold divinely revealed truth? How could a Church that claims to be holy protect or even enforce something as unholy and ungodly as slavery? Do those who make such objections have a case? Or is this one of those anti-Catholic fabrications?

Slavery as an Institution

Slavery in the Old Testament
There is no denying that slavery was an accepted fact in the Old Testament. In general, one could say that slaves were seen as an essential part of a Hebrew household. In the Old Testament we find two sets of laws regarding slaves: one set for Hebrew slaves (Lev. 25:38–42) and a second set for non-Hebrew slaves (Lev. 25:44–46).

> I, the LORD, am your God, who brought you out of the land of Egypt to give you the land of Canaan and to be your God. When your kindred with you, having been so reduced to poverty, sell themselves to you, do not make them work as slaves. Rather, let them be like laborers or like your tenants, working with you until the jubilee year, when, together with any children, they shall be released from your service and return to their family and to their ancestral property. Since they are my servants, whom I brought

3

out of the land of Egypt, they shall not sell themselves as slaves are sold.

The male and female slaves that you possess—these you shall acquire from the nations round about you. You may also acquire them from among the resident aliens who reside with you, and from their families who are with you, those whom they bore in your land. These you may possess, and bequeath to your children as their hereditary possession forever. You may treat them as slaves. But none of you shall lord it harshly over any of your fellow Israelites.

What is the difference between Hebrew slaves and non-Hebrew slaves? Hebrew slaves would become slaves either because of extreme poverty (in which case they could sell themselves to another Israelite) or because of inability to pay a debt. For non-Hebrew slaves, the situation was rather different. Most of them were prisoners of war. According to the Hebrew Bible, non-Hebrew slaves were drawn primarily from the neighboring Canaanite nations. A religious justification for the enslavement of these neighbors was based on a curse aimed at Canaan, a son of Ham. However, unlike other near-eastern faith-based laws, non-Hebrew slaves were not to do labor on the Sabbath and Festivals.

Clearly, the laws governing non-Hebrew slaves were harsher than those governing Hebrew slaves: non-Hebrew slaves could be owned permanently and bequeathed to the owner's children, whereas Hebrew slaves were treated as servants, and were released after seven years of service. In English translations of the Bible, the distinction is sometimes emphasized by translating the word as "slave" in the context of non-Hebrew slaves, and "servant" for Hebrew slaves.

Jeremiah (34:8–16) describes, in very forceful terms, how God punished the Israelites for not properly following the laws on slavery:

The word which came to Jeremiah from the LORD after King Zedekiah had made a covenant with all the people who were in Jerusalem to proclaim release to them: that each man should set free his male servant and each man his female servant, a Hebrew man or a Hebrew woman; so that no one should keep them, a Jew his brother, in bondage. And all the officials and all the people obeyed who had entered into the covenant that each man should set free his male servant and each man his female servant, so that no one should keep them any longer in bondage; they obeyed, and set them free. But afterward they turned around and took back the male servants and the female servants whom they had set free, and brought them into subjection for male servants and for female servants.

Then the word of the LORD came to Jeremiah from the LORD, saying, "Thus says the LORD God of Israel, 'I made a covenant with your forefathers in the day that I brought them out of the land of Egypt, from the house of bondage, saying, "At the end of seven years each of you shall set free his Hebrew brother who has been sold to you and has served you six years, you shall send him out free from you; but your forefathers did not obey Me or incline their ear to Me. Although recently you had turned and done what is right in My sight, each man proclaiming release to his neighbor, and you had made a covenant before Me in the house which is called by My name. Yet you turned and profaned My name, and each man took back his male servant and each man his female servant whom you had set free according to their desire, and you brought them into subjection to be your male servants and female servants.""""

The Old Testament does set minimum rules for the conditions under which slaves were to be kept. Slaves were to be treated as part of an extended family and were allowed to celebrate the Sukkot festival (Deut. 16:14). They were expected to honor Shabbat (Ex. 20:10). Hebrew slaves could not to be compelled to work with rigor (Lev. 25:43 and 53), and debtors who sold themselves as slaves to their creditors had to be treated the same as a hired servant (Lev. 25:39).

Sexual relations between a slave owner and female slaves were apparently acceptable in the time of the patriarchs, given the fact that children resulting from such liaisons were integrated into the patriarch's family. Sexual relations with slaves became prohibited in later eras (Lev. 19:20–22), but violations were reported even after prohibitions were instituted. The fact that certain forms of behavior were accepted in Old Testament times does not make them morally acceptable. Polygamy, divorce, prostitution, and eye-for-an-eye-revenge may have been common in Palestine, but soon Jesus would tell the Jews, "It was told to you . . . , but I tell you. . . ." The rule of "an eye for an eye" may have curbed more excessive forms of revenge, but it still could make the whole world blind—to paraphrase Gandhi.

To sum up, numerous passages in the Old Testament do justify slavery. But that is only part of the story. Slavery was also subject to certain conditions designed to ensure humane treatment and, under certain circumstances, even ultimate freedom. Nevertheless, slavery was part of Jewish life—in fact, part of ancient life in general. The Jews were surrounded by nations and cultures that had slaves. Slavery was an established and accepted fact, institutionally recognized by most societies.

For centuries, slavery was a powerful economic system. An often heard explanation for slavery is the following. Slavery entered human history with civilization. Hunter-gatherers and primitive farmers have no use for a slave. They collect or grow just enough food for themselves. In this kind of society, there is no economic advantage in owning another human being. But once societies become more concentrated and "civilized," the need for more food grows, and "extra hands" are very welcome. We do indeed see this phenomenon in history. When a town fell to a hostile army, it was normal to take into slavery those inhabitants who would make useful workers, and then kill the rest.

Does acceptance of the institution of slavery mean the Bible has lost its moral authority? I do not see how. Even if the Old Testament tacitly tolerated slavery, it certainly does not sanction it. Nowhere are we commanded to own slaves. An argument from silence does not connote approval.

The Roots of Slavery

What makes any discussion about slavery in the past much more complicated is that there are at least three different types of slavery.

First there is chattel slavery, also called traditional slavery. It is so named because people are treated as the personal property (chattel) of an owner and are bought and sold as if they were commodities.

This is how slavery is commonly understood and condemned today. Second, there is debt bondage or bonded slavery, which occurs when a person pledges himself or herself against a loan. Debt bondage can be passed on from generation to generation, with children required to pay off their parents' debt. It is a form of slavery that still exists in some societies as a way of paying a debt. Third, there is forced labor slavery; this occurs when an individual is forced to work against his or her will, under threat of violence or other punishment, with restrictions on their freedom. This form applies mostly to prisoners of war.

In the earliest known records, slavery in any of its forms is treated as an established institution. The Code of Hammurabi (c. 1760 BC), for example, prescribed death for anyone who helped a slave to escape or who sheltered a fugitive. Slavery was actually known in almost every ancient civilization and society surrounding Palestine, including Sumer, Egypt, China, the Akkadian Empire, Assyria, India, Greece, and the Roman Empire. This most likely explains why the Bible too mentions and accepts slavery as an established institution. Israel did not live in a vacuum.

Records of slavery in Ancient Greece go as far back as Mycenaean Greece. It is certain that Classical Athens had the largest slave population at the time, with as many as 80,000 in the 6th and 5th centuries BC; two- to four-fifths of the population were slaves. As the Roman Republic expanded outward, entire populations were enslaved, thus creating an ample supply from all over Europe and the Mediterranean. Slaves were considered property under Roman law and had no legal personhood. Greeks, Illyrians, Berbers, Germans, Britons, Thracians, Gauls, Arabs, and many more nationalities were slaves used not only for labor, but also for amusement (e.g., gladiators and sex slaves).

This also happened to Jews. Many Jews were taken to Rome as prisoners of war, but Julius Caesar, who was fairly friendly towards Judaism, appears to have freed most of them according to Tacitus and Suetonius. The Jewish historian Josephus, himself a former first century slave, remarks that the faithfulness of Jewish slaves was appreciated by their owners; this may have been one of the main reasons for freeing them.

Although the Roman Empire ultimately declined, slavery remained. Large-scale trading in slaves was mainly confined to the South and East of early medieval Europe: the Byzantine Empire and the Muslim world were the destinations for slaves from pagan Central and Eastern Europe. Viking, Arab, Greek, and Jewish merchants were all involved in the slave trade during the Early Middle Ages. The trade in European slaves reached a peak in the 10th century, especially due to Muslim slave traders.

Medieval Spain and Portugal were the scene of almost constant Muslim invasion of the predominantly Christian area. Periodic raiding expeditions were sent from Al-Andalus to ravage the Iberian Christian kingdoms, bringing back booty and slaves. In raids against Lisbon, Portugal in 1189, for example, the Almohad caliph Yaqub al-Mansur took 3,000 female and child captives, while his governor of Córdoba, in a subsequent attack upon the Portuguese town of Silves in 1191 took 3,000 Christian slaves. And this went on into the 19th century when North African Barbary pirates engaged in so-called *razzias*, raids on European coastal towns, to capture Christian slaves to sell at slave markets in places such as Algeria and Morocco.

Let us delve deeper into one of those perspectives—the aspect of slavery seen through a "moral eye." Most people nowadays agree that slavery is morally wrong. But I need to add another consideration here. Some people have claimed—and still claim—that slavery is not really a moral issue but a biological issue that would legitimize, for instance, the slave trade from Africa to the Americas. Their reasoning is that biological differences between people legitimize slavery—and that is where the moral aspect is supposed to end.

Let me explain the fallacy of this point of view with an example used by President Abraham Lincoln:

> If A. can prove, however conclusively, that he may, of right, enslave B.—why may not B. snatch the same argument, and prove equally, that he may enslave A?—You say A. is white, and B. is black. It is color, then; the lighter, having the right to enslave the darker? Take care. By this rule, you are to be slave to the first man you meet, with a fairer skin than your own. You mean the whites are intellectually the superiors of the blacks; and, therefore have the right to

enslave them? Take care again. By this rule, you are to be slave to the first man you meet, with an intellect superior to your own.

President Lincoln's point is well made and crystal clear: what some people come up with to defend the legitimacy of slavery is based on biological criteria such as a darker skin color or a lower intelligence. These standards are both relative and morally irrelevant. For, because those criteria are utterly relative, someone with a lighter skin or higher intelligence would then have the "moral right" to enslave you.

Moral values are absolute ends-in-themselves—not disposable means-to-other-ends. In morality, there is no "Thou shall not . . . , unless. . . ." Whereas our bodily movements are subject to physical constraints, our social actions are subject to moral ones. The only authority that can obligate us this way is something—or rather someone—infinitely superior to us; no one else has the right to demand our absolute obedience in matters of human dignity, human freedom, and the like. Moral rights and duties are absolute, objective standards of human behavior—they are non-negotiable. We are fully responsible for the moral choices we make in life.

Indeed, we do have a *choice* when it comes to morality, but that does not mean we can just pick whatever we want. A majority vote cannot determine the morality of slavery or abortion. Abraham Lincoln put it well when he challenged the Nebraska bill of 1820 that would let residents vote to decide if slavery would be legal in their territory: "God did not place good and evil before man, telling him to make his choice." There is no "pro-choice" in morality. Whatever we call legal must ultimately be judged by what is moral. Legally, we may have a choice, but morally we do not.

In general, we must acknowledge that slavery was an integral part of society during most of human history. The people of Palestine did not make an exemption. Hence, it should not surprise us that Christians inherited this "social," or rather a-social, phenomenon. They were surrounded by slavery and actually had many of their converts among slaves. How, then, did they come to see slavery as morally wrong?

Did Christians Ever Oppose Slavery?

Christians Were Surrounded by Slavery

Christianity was born in the cradle of Judaism, embedded in the framework of the Roman Empire. Jesus presented himself as a slave; slaves became saints in early Christendom; slavery became a metaphor and model for Christian life. During the first century, the time of the New Testament, slaves who converted to Christianity were regarded as freedman brothers and sisters in Christ—they were included in the inheritance of Christ's kingdom. These slaves were also told to serve their masters as if they were serving Christ—that is, with faithfulness and respectfulness (Eph. 6:5–8). Yet, slaves were still encouraged by St. Paul to seek or purchase their freedom whenever possible (1 Cor. 7:21).

Apparently, St. Paul put this issue in a much wider context: "There is neither Jew nor Greek, slave nor free, male nor female, for you are all one in Christ Jesus" (Gal. 3:28), suggesting that Christians take off these titles because they are now clothed in Christ (Gal. 3:27). In God's eyes, there is no place for such social distinctions. In the First Epistle to the Corinthians, Paul states (1 Cor. 7:21–24):

> Were you called while a slave? Do not worry about it; but if you are able also to become free, rather do that. For he who was called in the Lord while a slave, is the Lord's freedman; likewise he who was called while free, is Christ's slave. You were bought with a price; do not become slaves of men. Brethren, each one is to remain with God in that condition in which he was called.

In other words, whereas pagans make a distinction between two categories of people—slaves and non-slaves—Christians should not acknowledge such a distinction. Yet, when St. Paul (Philem. 1:16) wrote to the slave-owner Philemon about his runaway slave Onesimus, he did not say that Philemon was morally obliged to free Onesimus and any other slaves he may have had. Then St. Paul did say the following:

> Perhaps this was why he was parted from you for a while, that you might have him back forever, no longer as a slave but as more than a slave, as a beloved brother.

Obviously, there is some ambiguity in St. Paul's statements about slavery. He accepts slavery in the setting of society, but not within the Christian community. This may have effectively blocked the early Fathers of the Church from denouncing slavery outright, given that the Church considered Paul's text as inspired Scripture. St. John Chrysostom, for instance, in his sermon on Philemon, considers Paul's sending Onesimus back to his master a sign that slavery ought *not* to be abolished. Nevertheless, we should also note that, when Paul told slaves to obey their masters, he made no general defense of slavery, any more than he made a general defense of the pagan government of Rome, which Christians were also instructed to obey despite its injustices (cf. Rom. 13:1–7). He seems simply to have regarded slavery as an intractable part of the social order, an impermanent order that might very well pass away shortly (1 Cor. 7:29–31).

Yet Paul's ambivalence did influence what followed. Most Christian figures in the next centuries of Christianity—people such as St. Augustine—accepted slavery as a fact, although they did not explicitly support it. Augustine described slavery and private property not as the creations of God but of *sin*. Needless to say, he has been criticized for apparently accepting the cultural *status quo* instead of challenging it—as he never really questioned the institution of slavery.

Augustine's first mention of the topic is in one of his letters when he saw the slave trade in Africa:

> There are so many of those in Africa who are commonly called "slave dealers" (mangones), that they seem to be draining Africa of much of its human population and transferring their "merchandise" to provinces across the sea.

Although St. Augustine does have some critical words about slavery, he does not touch the institution as such. Should his Christian beliefs not have given him the courage to attack the institution? For some reason, they did not. Perhaps he just happened to be a child of his time, unable to shake off what is wrong with the society he belonged to. Perhaps he just considered slavery a consequence of original sin. Perhaps he could not refer to any statement of Jesus that condemned slavery—in contrast to statements of Jesus in which he condemned another institution, divorce. This poses the question, of course, why Jesus never addressed slavery. Why did Jesus not say "It was told to you . . . , but I tell you. . . ."? Usually, Jesus responded to questions that Pharisees asked him. Somehow, slavery was not a question for them, hence the lack of response or formulation against slavery.

The fact remains, though, that St. Augustine did not condemn slavery. It would take many more years before Catholics began to see more clearly its intrinsic evil. Why did it take so long? One of the main reasons is that Christian morals were considered to be for Christians, not non-Christians—in other words, Christians were supposed not to treat each other as slaves, but that did not apply to the rest of society. This "rule" would remain in effect at least until the entire society became Christian under Emperor Constantine. To put it in a simplified phrase, slavery was considered un-Christian but not un-civilized.

In retrospect, it is easy to reproach the Church of the first ages for not having condemned slavery in principle, and for having tolerated it as a fact. But we should also realize that slavery was a cornerstone of society at that time. Had the Church stirred up a frightful revolution—if it would have had the power to do so, which is very doubtful—perhaps Roman society would have collapsed, and with it all civilization around it.

The fact remains that neither Jesus nor his followers directly challenged the institution of slavery. The Fathers of the Church actually accepted the buying, selling and owning of human beings even by Christians, as did the popes (Muslim slaves were manning papal galleys until 1800) as well as religious orders (Jesuits in colonial Maryland owned slaves, as did nuns in Europe and Latin America). Even St. Peter Claver, who in Colombia befriended, instructed, and baptized African slaves, bought slaves to serve as interpreters. In general, we could say that Church leaders challenged abuses of slaveholding but rarely the practice itself.

Yet, there was a growing sentiment that slavery was not compatible with Christian conceptions of charity and justice. How could the Church deal with this ambiguous problem? One of the ways was by declaring slavery as "unjust" if it is a form of involuntary servitude in which a human being is regarded as no more than the property of another, as being without basic human rights—in other words, as a thing rather than a person. In this form of slavery, the slave ceases to be (or never was) a legal person and so has no rights as a person, cannot legally marry, and may be sold away from home and relatives. But in contrast to this form of slavery, Christians also acknowledged something like "just servitude" in which a metaphysical distinction is made between owning a *person* as an object, and only owning the *work* of that person. This is a distinction we could even apply to our current labor force in modern society.

Nevertheless, the Christian Church, from very early in its history, treated slaves as persons, and they were allowed to be baptized, marry, and also be ordained. Even though slavery was not altogether repudiated, slaves and free men had equal access to the sacraments, and many clerics were from slave backgrounds, including two popes (Pius I and Callixtus I). This implies a fundamental equality that cannot possibly be compatible with slavery. One could even make the case that this difference in legal status in the long term undermined the whole position of slavery.

In spite of some horrible violations, Roman Catholic teaching began to steadily evolve by turning more strongly against "unjust" forms of slavery in general, prohibiting the enslavement of the recently baptized, culminating in pronouncements by Pope Paul III in 1537. The Church did succeed in almost entirely enforcing that a free Christian could not be enslaved, for example when being a captive in war. In the Bull *Sublimus Dei* (1537), Pope Paul III forbade "unjust" kinds of enslavement relating to the indigenous peoples of the Americas and all other people. The Pontiff characterized enslavers as allies of the devil and declared attempts to justify such slavery "null and void":

> The exalted God loved the human race so much that He created man in such a condition that he was not only a sharer in good as are other creatures, but also that he would be able to reach and see face to face the inaccessible and invisible Supreme Good. . . . Seeing this and envying it, the enemy of the human race, who always opposes all good men so that the race may perish, has thought up

a way, unheard of before now, by which he might impede the saving word of God from being preached to the nations. He (Satan) has stirred up some of his allies who, desiring to satisfy their own avarice, are presuming to assert far and wide that the Indians . . . be reduced to our service like brute animals, under the pretext that they are lacking the Catholic faith. And they reduce them to slavery, treating them with afflictions they would scarcely use with brute animals . . . by our Apostolic Authority decree and declare by these present letters that the same Indians and all other peoples—even though they are outside the faith—. . . should not be deprived of their liberty. . . . Rather they are to be able to use and enjoy this liberty and this ownership of property freely and licitly, and are not to be reduced to slavery.

Unfortunately, the Council of The West Indies and the Spanish Crown concluded that papal documents like these broke the rights that gave them a free hand in missionizing. Therefore, the pope withdrew those documents, though they continued to circulate and be quoted by those who supported Indian rights.

It is hard, if not impossible, to find a Father or Doctor of the Church who was an unqualified abolitionist. No pope or council, until very recently, ever made a sweeping condemnation of slavery as such. Yet they constantly sought to alleviate the evils of slavery and repeatedly denounced the mass enslavement of conquered populations and the infamous slave trade, thereby undermining slavery at its sources.

Therefore, the change of the Church's attitude toward slavery reflects the changed circumstances of the world more than it reflects any revolution in moral theology. The Church had done no more than proclaim that in other sets of social and historical circumstances, slavery represented the lesser of evils. But, admittedly, the lesser evil is still evil. This is not to whitewash the Church's history of slavery, but to set it within in a much wider context.

Is all of this disturbing? In a sense, it is. The Catholic Church believes she was founded by Jesus Christ, the Son of God, to proclaim and uphold divinely revealed truth. Therefore, we should evaluate how the Church, in particular her leadership, fared when confronted with the evil of slavery. Apparently, she neglected to take a firm stand against all forms of slavery for a long time. Fortunately, some of her best leaders and members did take a stand (as we will see in the next chapter). But that is the best we can say.

Was the Church wrong here and thus deserving of criticism? Certain moral doctrines are now seen as wrong because the course of history has demonstrated their error. It is through social changes that it became possible for Christians to overcome the blindness that had previously afflicted their moral vision. In other words, these moral rules had not reached the level of development we know now. People can only be judged according to the moral standards they know.

The Church may have made poor assessments regarding slavery, but never has she reversed her teaching. One could even say that a Church that admits that some of its past moral teachings were inadequate need not fear loss of moral authority any more than does a parent who admits to mistakes in childrearing or a judicial system that allows for appeals.

Beacons of Light

As we have seen, the Church initially accepted, or at least tolerated, slavery as a social institution during antiquity and even into the early Medieval period. She inherited the institution of slavery from outside herself. Yet, dissenting figures, although initially solitary, gradually began to appear on the Catholic scene by embracing abolitionism. The roots of abolitionism can be traced back to the Church's practice of baptizing slaves and treating them as human beings equal in dignity to all others. Somehow, the Christian attitude was beginning to infiltrate the surrounding society. Here are some highlights.

> In AD 54, Onesimus, the freed runaway slave whose master was Philemon, becomes third bishop of Byzantium, according to Eastern Orthodox Church tradition.

> Around AD 90, Pope Clement I observes how a certain form of slavery can be used to help others: "We know many among ourselves who have given themselves up to bonds, in order that they might ransom others. Many, too, have surrendered themselves to

slavery, that with the price which they received for themselves, they might provide food for others."

Apparently, slavery had become a means of charity for some. At the same time, St. Polycarp and St. Ignatius, second-generation Christian leaders, freed their slaves. In addition, a Roman prefect named Hermas received baptism at an Easter festival with his wife, children, and twelve hundred and fifty slaves. On that occasion, he gave all his slaves their freedom and generous gifts besides.

AD 95: Ovidius, appointed bishop of Braga (in modern day Portugal) under Pope Clement I, emancipates five thousand slaves.

AD 208–258: St. Cyprian of Carthage condemns slaveholding.

AD 315: Two years after issuing the Edict of Milan, legalizing Christianity, Emperor Constantine imposed the death penalty on those who kidnap and enslave children. He later forbid separating slave families and eased the conditions of the liberation process so that slaveholders could simply go to a church service and declare the liberation of their slaves before the bishop. Since Constantine was a new Christian, this suggests that the Christian community had a strong anti-slavery position, which was going to affect the surrounding society.

AD 379: St. Gregory of Nyssa, in a sermon during Lent, reminds his audience, "Since God's greatest gift to us is the perfect liberty vouchsafed us by Christ's saving action in time, and since God's gifts are entirely irrevocable, it lies not even in God's power to enslave men and women." In addition, he says that God has given dominion over the creation to each person, thus the possession of a slave as a material possession is contrary to creation.

AD 380: St. John Chrysostom declares, "Slavery is the fruit of covetousness, of extravagance, of insatiable greediness," and he also questioned what price could be put on a human soul.

AD 390–400: The *Apostolic Constitutions*, a summary of Christian teaching, directs Christians as follows: "As for such sums of money as are collected from them in the aforesaid manner, designate them to be used for the redemption of the saints and the deliverance of slaves and captives."

AD 395: St. Augustine, bishop of Hippo, notes that the Christian community regularly used its funds to redeem as many kidnapped victims as possible, and had recently purchased and freed 120 slaves whom the Galatians were boarding onto their ships.

AD 450: St. Patrick, himself a former slave, argues for the abolition of slavery.

AD 600: St. Eligius uses his vast wealth to purchase British and Saxon slaves in groups of 50 and 100 in order to set them free.

AD 600: St. Isidore of Seville declares that, "God has made no difference between the soul of the slave and that of the freedman." Once it was recognized that slaves had a soul just as did their masters, it could not forever be justified that they be another person's chattel.

AD 649: Clovis II, king of the Franks, marries a slave who later began a campaign to halt the traffic in slaves. The Catholic Church now honors her as St. Bathilda. She was canonized in 880 by Pope Nicholas I—in part for her efforts to free slaves and end the slave trade.

AD 801–865: St. Ansgar, Archbishop of Bremen, Germany, campaigns vigorously against slavery, freeing those the Vikings had captured, asserting the freedom of all of God's creation. When a number of Christians had been carried off as slaves by some of the pagan tribes in the north, St. Ansgar went at once to the chiefs who were responsible and, after an impassioned appeal, persuaded them to release all their captives.

AD 1000: St. Stephen, the first King of Hungary, officially abolishes slavery.

AD 1062: St. Wulfstan, Bishop of Worcester, campaigns vigorously against the slave trade based in the city of Bristol. At the time, those people who could not pay their debts were sold into slavery in Ireland. St. Wulfstan spent time in Bristol, preached sermons attacking slavery, so eventually slaves held captive in Bristol were released.

AD 1102: St. Anselm was another powerful Church leader to take a public stand against the slave trade. At a church council in St.

Peter's church, Westminster, he obtains the passage of a resolution against the practice of selling human beings like cattle.

It should be mentioned that the Middle Ages also witnessed the emergence of Societies and clerical Orders that had been founded for the purpose of freeing Christian slaves. The best known of these are the Trinitarian Order and the Mercedarians. The Trinitarians were founded in France in 1198 by St. John of Matha, with the original aim of ransoming captives in the crusades. The Mercedarians are an order of friars founded in Barcelona in 1218 by St. Peter Nolasco, whose particular original mission was the saving of Christian slave-captives in the wars between Christian Aragon and Muslim Spain (Al-andalus). Both operated by collecting money to redeem the captives, and organizing the business of buying them back.

Another beacon of light was St. Vincent de Paul (1581–1660). He had been captured by Barbary corsairs and enslaved for some years before escaping. He used his position as chaplain to the aristocrat in charge of the French galley fleet to run missions among the slaves and improve their conditions, but he went short of seriously challenging the galley-slave system itself.

Throughout this period the popes were far from silent. As soon as the enslavement of native populations by European colonists started, they began to protest. During the 1430s, the Spanish colonized the Canary Islands and began to enslave the native population. This was not serfdom but true slavery of the sort that Christians and Moors had long practiced upon one another's captives in Spain. When word of these actions reached Pope Eugene IV, he issued his 1435 bull *Sicut Dudum*. The pope did not mince words. Under threat of excommunication, he gave everyone involved fifteen days from receipt of his bull:

> to restore to their earlier liberty all and each person of either sex who were once residents of said Canary Islands. . . . These people are to be totally and perpetually free and are to be let go without the exaction or reception of any money.

Pius II and Sixtus IV emphatically repeated these prohibitions. And, as noted above, in a Bull addressed to all the faithful of the Christian world, Pope Paul III in 1537 condemned the enslavement of Indians in North and South America. Special mention in this context should be made of the Dominican Friar Bartolomé de las Casas, the first resident Bishop of Chiapas (1474–1566), who was instrumental in compelling the Spanish crown to enact a law in 1542 prohibiting the enslavement of the Indians—the first country in the world to do so. He chronicled one of the sermons of his confrere Antonio de Montesino:

> These [Indians], are they not men? Do they not have rational souls? Are you not obligated to love them as you love yourselves? Do you not understand this? Do you not feel this? How is it that you are in such a deep, lethargic sleep? You can be sure that in your state you are no more able to be saved than the Moors or Turks, who lack and don't even want the faith of Jesus Christ.

A number of popes would follow by issuing papal bulls condemning enslavement and mistreatment of Native Americans by Spanish and Portuguese colonials; however, these were largely ignored despite the threat of excommunication. Unfortunately, the official view of a Church does not always easily trickle down to her members. A phrase, so often used by Catholics, does not always come true: "*Roma locuta est, causa finita est*" ("Rome has spoken, the case is closed"). The case of slavery certainly was not closed. Many more declarations had to come before people "at the base" would accept that slavery was evil, and the case could finally be closed.

Here are a few major steps before the case could be "closed." In his decree *Cum Sicuti*, dated April 18, 1591, Gregory XIV ordered reparations to be made by Catholics in the Philippines to the natives, who had been forced into slavery by Europeans, and he commanded, under pain of excommunication of the owners, that all native slaves in the islands be set free. Urban VIII in 1639 issued a Bull applying the principles of Paul III to Portuguese colonies in South America and requiring the liberation of all Indian slaves. In 1741 Pope Benedict XIV promulgated the papal Bull *Immensa Pastorum Principis* against the enslavement of the indigenous peoples of the Americas and other countries. In 1815 Pope Pius VII demanded of the Congress of Vienna the suppression of the slave trade.

Thus it was no real break with previous teaching when Gregory XVI and Leo XIII issued a general condemnation of slavery—in particular, the importation of Negro slaves from Africa. Pope Gregory's 1839 Bull *In Supremo Apostolatus* was not only aimed at slave trading, but it also clearly condemned any kind of racial slavery:

> [We] admonish and adjure in the Lord all believers in Christ, of whatsoever condition, that no one hereafter may dare unjustly to molest Indians, Negroes, or other men of this sort; or to spoil them of their goods; or to reduce them to slavery; or to extend help or favor to others who perpetuate such things against them; or to excuse that inhuman trade by which Negroes, as if they were not men, but mere animals, howsoever reduced to slavery, are, without any distinction, contrary to the laws of justice and humanity, bought, sold, and doomed sometimes to the most severe and exhausting labors.

In the 1888 Bull of *Canonization of Peter Claver*, one of the most illustrious adversaries of slave trading, Pope Leo XIII branded the "supreme villainy" of the slave traders. He also condemned slavery in his Encyclical *In Plurimis*:

> In the presence of so much suffering, the condition of slavery, in which a considerable part of the great human family has been sunk in squalor and affliction now for many centuries, is deeply to be deplored; for the system is one which is wholly opposed to that which was originally ordained by God and by nature. The Supreme Author of all things so decreed that man should exercise a sort of royal dominion over beasts and cattle and fish and fowl, but never that men should exercise a like dominion over their fellow men.

Finally, it was at the Second Vatican Council in 1965 that the Catholic Church, categorically and unconditionally, categorized slavery as intrinsically *evil*, meaning that it is evil in every circumstance in and of itself (*Gaudium et Spes*):

> Furthermore, whatever is opposed to life itself, such as any type of murder, genocide, abortion, euthanasia or wilful self-destruction, whatever violates the integrity of the human person, such as mutilation, torments inflicted on body or mind, attempts to coerce the

will itself; whatever insults human dignity, such as subhuman living conditions, arbitrary imprisonment, deportation, slavery,
prostitution, the selling of women and children; as well as dis-
graceful working conditions, where men are treated as mere tools
for profit, rather than as free and responsible persons; all these
things and others of their like are infamies indeed. They poison
human society, but they do more harm to those who practice
them than those who suffer from the injury. Moreover, they are
supreme dishonor to the Creator.

Did all these official statements from the Catholic Church help
the case against slavery? Unfortunately, individual members of the
Church do not always live by Church teachings. Nowadays, for
instance, the Church's position is categorically pro-life and against
abortion, but that does not mean that all her members take that
stand too. The same can be said about slavery. It had been part of
society for so long and it had been propelled by such strong greed
that the final abolition of slavery did not come easily.

There may have been only a few lonely voices in the desert pro-
testing against slavery and slave trading, but at least they were beacons of light in the surrounding darkness. What most were not able
to see, these people could see more or less clearly, so they could help
others in the Church—and finally in society—also to see more and
more clearly what is wrong with slavery. Apparently the record of
Catholic abolitionism is not as poor as many myths want us to
believe. But neither, we should note, is it an altogether pretty story.

Did Catholic Morals Change?

A Change, but of What?

The burning question, of course, is did Catholic morals change over
time, from condoning slavery to opposing slavery? The answer is
yes and no. Yes, the moral *evaluations* about slavery may have
changed, but it is not the moral *value* of human dignity and freedom that changed over time. Such a distinction is important to
make.

Moral evaluations are our *personal* feelings or discernments
regarding values. Moral evaluations may change, but moral values

do not. Evaluations are subjective and relative, whereas values are objective and absolute. Evaluations concern someone's personal attitude toward moral values, causing some to think that morality is merely a matter of evaluations determined by special interest groups or a majority vote. However, the value itself ("being a value") is not relative but absolute, and should be distinguished from human attitudes toward values ("being valued").

Nonetheless, many people think that "having value" is the same as "being valued." In so doing, they hold that by making evaluations, we create values in accordance with these evaluations. So when evaluations change, the moral values and laws are believed to change as well. If that were true, even moral values would be a matter of utter relativity, depending on the era, culture, and location of the person who makes these evaluations. The result is a real confusion. Think of this comparison with physics: it is not the law of gravity that has changed in the history of science, but our understanding of it certainly has. Obviously, we shouldn't confuse our current understanding of physical laws with the way those laws really are as we may find out some day. In a similar vein, do not confuse our current moral evaluations with the moral laws and values themselves. Moral truths do not change, even though times may change.

If this is so, one might wonder how we could ever have access to objective values if our subjective evaluations keep changing. Thinking that subjective evaluations are all there is leads easily to what they call "moral relativism." This is the viewpoint held by relativists; ironically, though, their stance amounts to an absolute claim stating that there are no absolutes (except for this absolute claim itself, of course). Relativists reject any authority, yet they want to be the new authority by proclaiming the absolute truth that there are no absolute truths. According to their rationale, anyone who disagrees with them must be misinformed. For them, all we have are moral evaluations, but there are no eternal moral laws and values.

As a result, relativists consider themselves in charge of the moral terminology that we use, so they can manipulate it according to their needs. They replace, for instance, the old term "abortion" with the new term "selective reproduction." They determine what the term "human" means by demarcating whoever qualifies for this predicate: perhaps only those who are not slaves, only Aryans, only the biologically fit, only those who have left the womb, or those who have not become a burden to society. From then on, everything becomes relative to the criteria relativists invent on the spot, all by themselves by making them sound "politically correct."

The Catholic Church takes the side of moral absolutists, who emphasize that evaluations are merely a reflection of the way we discern moral values at the current time and react to them—in other words, moral evaluations may change but moral values will not. Absolutists want to stress that moral values and laws are eternal, objective, and absolute. Whereas relativists won't acknowledge the possibility of making moral mistakes, absolutists certainly would, because there are absolute and eternal standards by which to judge our actions. Relativists would say that slavery was not always wrong but was gradually seen as wrong. Absolutists would say that slavery was always wrong, even when we did not discern it yet as wrong—which would then be a moral mistake.

In the same way as scientists, moralists are "absolutists": they are ultimately in search of absolute, objective laws, but they realize they may not be there yet. As C. S. Lewis once put it, "The human mind has no more power of inventing a new value than of imagining a new primary color." Just as we may be oblivious to laws of nature not yet discovered, we also may violate moral laws of which we are not aware. Truth is not a personal item determined by personal feelings. I can only proclaim "the" truth, but there is no such thing as "my" truth.

It is the Church's task to make us aware of those eternal moral values and laws. First of all, there is what is called the "natural law," which finds its biblical roots in St. Paul's reference to pagans "who never heard of the Law but are led by reason to do what the Law commands" (Rom. 2:14). This is something like a "moral common sense." St. Thomas Aquinas describes the natural law as "the light of understanding placed in us by God; through it we know what we must do and what we must avoid. God has given this light or law at the creation," according to the Catechism of the Catholic Church (CCC 1955). The Ten Commandments come to us from the outside and complete the interior knowledge of the natural law that has become obscured. The Ten Commandments did not originate from a majority vote, and cannot be changed by a poll. As President Ronald Reagan once said, "I have wondered at times about what the Ten Commandments would have looked like if Moses had run them through the U.S. Congress."

How then could it be possible that we do not always see what is right or wrong? The answer is that we are sinners who can be blinded by our emotions, passions, and lusts. That is why we may be temporarily "blind" in our evaluations when it comes to matters of morals, moral values, and moral laws. Nevertheless, some among us are able to clearly discern certain moral values and evaluate them properly, whereas others are not. Only a few people in the past were able to discern the objective, intrinsic, and universal value of personal freedom and human rights (versus slavery), whereas most of their contemporaries were blind for this value. Moral laws are intrinsically right, even when we do not see yet that they are. Anyone who does not see their evidence is morally blind. Just like there are color-blind people, there are also value-blind people. Just as science has its geniuses, morality has its sages—just think of people such as Moses, the Prophets, and the Saints. In the previous chapter, I gave you a list of some "beacons of light" in the slavery debate.

Undoubtedly, the Christian principles of charity ("Love your neighbor as yourself") and the Golden Rule ("Do unto others as you would have them to do unto you") espoused by the Scriptures are ultimately incompatible with chattel slavery, even if, because of its deeply established role as a social institution, this point was not clearly understood by all at the time. The Seventh Commandment in particular forbids acts that lead "to the enslavement of human beings, to their being bought, sold and exchanged like merchandise, in disregard for their personal dignity" (CCC 2414). It is no wonder, then, that St. Paul directed a Christian master to treat his Christian slave "no longer as a slave but more than a slave, as a beloved brother, . . . both in the flesh and in the Lord" (Philem. 1:16).

Slowly but surely, the Church would develop a clearer understanding of what is morally wrong with slavery—and has always been wrong. St. Augustine is a clear example of someone who did not condemn slavery yet, but was on his way to discerning the ultimate truth about slave raiding and human trafficking when he wrote these words:

> But who resists these traders who are found everywhere, who traffic, not in animals but in human beings, not in barbarians but in Romans from the provinces? Who resists when these people from everywhere and from every side, carried off by violence and ensnared by deception, are led away into the hands of those who bid for them? Who will resist in the name of Roman freedom—I shall not say, the common freedom, but their very own?
>
> Even if I wished to list all the crimes—just the ones we have had contact with—it would not be possible to do so. . . . There was not lacking a faithful Christian who, knowing our custom in missions of mercy of this kind, made this known to the church. Immediately, partially from the ship in which they had already been loaded, partially from the spot where they had been hidden prior to boarding, about 120 were freed by our people, though I myself was absent. Scarcely five or six were found to have been sold by their parents; of all the others, hardly a person could keep himself from tears on hearing all the various ways by which they were brought to the Galatians by trickery and kidnapping."

The Allied war-crimes court that tried the Nazi leadership after World War II was sharply aware of this problem. The tribunal could not bring these men to justice on the basis of German law, for they had been empowered to commit their crimes by the elected government of Germany. Nor was there any real evidence that the German people had somehow withdrawn their consent. In the end, the tribunal had to judge Nazi leaders on the basis of such considerations as "the elementary dictates of humanity." Catholics would say "on the basis of natural law." Martin Luther King Jr. was right when he called an unjust (legal) law "a code that is out of harmony with the moral law." The law of the land is not always a reflection of the moral law.

The Yeast of Society

This takes us to the following question: what is the relationship between the morals of the Church and the morals of society? Let me say first that it is at the core of Christianity that we separate the two—Church vs. Society, Church vs. State, or Religion vs. Politics.

Ancient history is replete with examples of the mixing and melding of Church and State. Typically a successful ruler or king would assume various "priestly" titles in addition to the "temporal" titles that such a position tended to confer. Examples of mixing and melding these opposites are numerous. The execution of Socrates was one of them, whereby the philosopher was sentenced to death by the Athenian state for, among other things, "his disrespect for the gods." Or take the claim of many of the ancient kings of Judah to rule with a mandate from Heaven, or the Edict of Thessalonica, whereby Nicene Christianity was made the state church of the Roman Empire.

In Benedict XVI's discussion of the separation of religion and politics in his book *Jesus of Nazareth* (Part II, p. 170), he writes: "In his teaching and in his whole ministry, Jesus had inaugurated a non-political Messianic kingdom and had begun to detach these two hitherto inseparable realities from one another." And elsewhere (Part I, p. 40) he says that, when the two fuse, "faith becomes the servant of power and must bend to its criteria." In the words of Jesus, render to Caesar what is Caesar's, but never render to Caesar what is God's. On the one hand, the Church depends on the State to keep and enforce justice. On the other hand, the State depends on religious conviction, which makes people respond to each other in a moral and respectful way. Because of this relationship, Church and State are not in opposition to one another, but complement each other and need each other.

This explains why Jesus did not explore issues of a purely political nature, as his Kingdom is not of this world. Is slavery perhaps such a political issue? However, slavery is more than political—Jesus became a slave himself, who washed the feet of his disciples. Applying Jesus's basic principle of Church-State relations—"give to Caesar what is Caesar's and to God what is God's" (Mk. 12:17)—Catholic teaching has always recognized an indispensable role for government in human affairs and instructed the faithful to honor political authority, but it has also insisted that the power of the State has limits and that the freedom of individuals, the Church, and other institutions must be respected by political officials (CCC 2234–2246).

How different, though, is reality. Once Christianity had become the leading religion of the Roman Empire, monarchs would rule their empires by the idea of "divine right." Sometimes this divine right began to be used by a monarch to support the notion that the king ruled both his own kingdom and the Church within its boundaries, a theory known as caesaropapism. Centuries later, in 1555, this idea became the principle that the religion of the ruler is that of the people (*cuius regio, eius religio*).

On the other side was the Catholic doctrine that the pope, as the Vicar of Christ on earth, should have the ultimate authority over the Church, and indirectly over the State. In the year 494, Pope Gelasius I writes to Emperor Anastasius:

> There are two powers, august Emperor, by which this world is chiefly ruled, namely, the sacred authority of the priests and the royal power. Of these that of the priests is the weightier, since they have to render an account for even the kings of men in the divine judgment. You are also aware, dear son, that while you are permitted honorably to rule over humankind, yet in things divine you bow your head humbly before the leaders of the clergy and await from their hands the means of your salvation. In the reception and proper disposition of the heavenly mysteries you recognize that you should be subordinate rather than superior to the religious order, and that in these matters you depend on their judgment rather than wish to force them to follow your will.

It did not always work this way. The issue of the separation of Church and State during the medieval period centered on monarchs who ruled in the secular sphere but encroached on the Church's rule of the spiritual sphere. This unresolved contradiction in ultimate control of the Church led to power struggles and crises of leadership. The old notion that Church and State are two independent realms, one secular and one spiritual, had to be inaugurated again by Pope Gregory VII. He is best known for the part he played in the so-called Investiture Controversy, in which he confronted Henry IV, Holy Roman Emperor, and affirmed the primacy of papal authority and the new canon law governing the election of the pope by the College of Cardinals. Henry insisted that he reserved the traditionally established right of previous emperors to "invest" bishops and other clergymen, despite the papal decree. Ultimately, this controversy was resolved in the Concordat of Worms in 1122. By this concordat, the emperor renounced the right to invest ecclesiastics with ring and crosier, the symbols of their spiritual power, and guaranteed election by the canons of cathedral or abbey and free consecration.

After the Reformation, some states tried again to impose new regulations on churches; the control of religion was handed over again to the rulers of the State. The religious conflicts were mitigated in 1555 as part of the Peace of Augsburg by the principle of *cuius regio, eius religio*. In reaction to situations in which the religion of the individual was made to depend almost totally upon the society into which one was born, the United States decided to separate the Church from the State again and gave everyone the right to choose whatever religion—or lack of religion—one wishes, without any control of the State. The reason behind this separation of Church and State is the free exercise of religion—a principle that aims not at protecting the State from Religion but at protecting Religion from the State.

Obviously, the battle for the separation of Church and State is a timeless issue and needs constant attention. An important new step in this process was the introduction of a new Code of Canon Law in 1917. It was Pope Leo XIII who recognized that the Church's future rested in her independence as a moral and spiritual power. Thus the Church stepped back from more than a millennium of close association with State power. Eventually this would lead to the systemization of canon law in the 1917 Code. No longer was the Church's internal life ordered by a patchwork of old canon law that often combined sacred and secular authority. Now the Church's law was entirely her own.

What does all of this have to do with slavery? At the birth of Christianity, Christians lived in a State that distinguished slaves from non-slaves and, at the same time, they were part of a Church that rejected such a distinction. There was a tension here between the secular morals of the State and the religious morals of the Church. Such a tension seems to be part and parcel of the relationship between Church and State. Only a clear separation can strengthen both sides—Christian morals do not always coincide with society's morals, so legal, secular laws may not always follow the moral law.

What is the role of the Church in this relationship? It is the Church's task to be the conscience of society. So when it comes to religious morals and secular morals, the Church should always correct, or at least question, the secular morals of the State as to whether they are in accordance with the religious morals of the Church, or whether the legal law is in harmony with the moral law. Has the Church always taken this task seriously? Unfortunately, she often just *reflected* the secular morals, whereas she should have *corrected* them. Christian morals—I mean the absolute and timeless ones, not necessarily the current ones—should be the ultimate standard to judge society's morals. If this view is correct, then the Church should not *reflect* but rather *correct* the morality of society. The Church should be the yeast of society as well as its conscience. However, she cannot really direct, but only inspect, the morality of society. In the words of Pope John Paul II, "The Church proposes; she imposes nothing."

Perhaps too often, though, the Church did not suggest good religious morals to society. Why not? The best we can say is that the Church had taken on the morals of the State as her own morals, instead of correcting them with the morals of the Church. It is not easy to shake off the "dust of society." The Church may not always be able to *impose* her own morals, but often she did not even try to *propose* those morals. All too often we tend to accept the rules of society instead of questioning them. That is why Jesus can say "It was told to you . . . , but I tell you. . . ."

Social institutions such as slavery can be accepted as a given, or they can be questioned by a higher moral authority. Ironically, even moral relativists hold on to at least one absolute moral authority that says "Never disobey your own conscience." So we should ask them the question as to where the absolute authority of a human conscience comes from. If our conscience were merely a private issue that we form at our own discretion, it could never claim any absolute authority, for moral disagreements cannot be settled on the level of a person's private and personal conscience. It is the

Church's task to be that authority. She needs to transform the world, not to be transformed by the world.

Has the Catholic Church always been that authority? Early Christians were always very reluctant to impose their Christian morals on the surrounding society. They tried to live by example—by the way they treated slaves in their midst—not by legislation—by ruling how everyone should live and act. They had no power to tell society what to do. Later on, when Christianity became the dominant religion, things would gradually, or even abruptly, change, and they would feel more responsible for the society they lived in.

Did the Church actually play her new role responsibly? Some may question whether she did, but I want to remark that the actual, current morals do not necessarily represent the ideal—they are "less than ideal." This has always been the case, even in the Old Testament. Jesus made this point very clearly when he said that—due to the hardness of ancient Israel's heart—God tolerated (and regulated) some things under the Old Law that he did not endorse. As God did so, however, he progressively revealed his divine will to mankind, clarifying his will more fully through Jesus Christ. Many of the injunctions found in the Old Testament pertaining to slavery fall into the same category—the category of regulating something that was "less than ideal."

Did Church Teaching Change?

Is There a Biblical Foundation?

As we found out so far, moral values may not have changed, but Church evaluations about slavery certainly have. Is it possible for the Church to hide behind her short-term evaluations in order to evade the timeless moral issue of slavery? The anti-Catholic myths around slavery make us believe the Church is just hiding the truth. But is she?

The problem the Church is confronted with is that it cannot fall back on a strong biblical basis regarding slavery, for the Bible does not really condemn slavery. Is that the end of the story? I don't think so. Let me say this first: the fact that something is or is not in the Bible is not the decisive point. The fact that the word "Trinity," for instance, is not in the Bible does not mean it is unbiblical. It was St. Augustine himself who acknowledged how things can change in morals and doctrine. Our understanding of what is in the Bible is in a process of development that St. Augustine describes as follows in his *Confessions* (XII, 31, 42):

> I am convinced that when he [Moses] wrote those words what he meant and what he thought was all the truth we have been able to discover there, and whatever truth we have not been able to find, or have not found yet, but which is nonetheless there to be found.

Especially since the Reformation, we often hear that the Bible is our main and sole guide—*Sola Scriptura*—which means that our faith is only defined by Scripture, not by Church tradition and Church interpretation as well. However, the notion of *Sola Scriptura* is an egg without a shell, so to speak. When St. Paul was preaching the Gospel, he was not carrying a book of four gospels around; such a book did just not exist at the time. To him and other early Christians, Scripture meant the Old Testament. In the meantime, the New Testament was in the making, right in the middle of the living Church.

So how did the New Testament come along and what determined which books should be included in it? This is the issue of the canon of the Bible. Many questions abound. Should the Jewish Scriptures be part of the Christian canon? The answer of the early Christian Church was a definite yes. All of them? Whereas the Jews did not accept the Books of the Maccabees in their canon, Christians did because those had played an important role in their own circles. It was not Scripture that decided this. And what should be in the canon of the New Testament? The tradition of the Church omitted a few Gospels of gnostic origin because they went against her tradition and were not used in her liturgies. Martin Luther would reject even more books, particularly the Letter of St. James, because it went against his *Sola Gratia* stand. We should be careful, though, not to use a certain scriptural canon to form a set of doctrines, then use this set of doctrines to prove our scriptural canon.

Before the idea of a "canon" of the New Testament had been formulated, the Church had already developed a different concept of what was canonical. The scriptures of the Old Testament needed a canon of New Testament interpretation—a living interpretation by means of the faith handed down from the apostles, which was the tradition of the *apostolic succession*. Scripture is not an entity in itself. It is a product of tradition—the tradition of the apostolic succession. Any text, even a text in Scripture, can have multiple interpretations. So Scripture cannot be interpreted by itself. As St. Thomas Aquinas used to say: "It is the task of the good interpreter to look, not at the words, but at the meaning."

Hence the question is: who determines what the correct interpretation is? The Catholic answer is to point to what the tradition determines—the same tradition that produced the text and handed it on through the apostolic succession. If it is not the Church who determines the correct interpretation, we end up with multiple denominations which keep splitting into smaller and smaller segments, each with its own interpretation of the Bible. It is not up to each individual Christian to determine which books should or should not be included in Scripture. The Bible is a book that came from the very heart of the Church; the Apostles authored and the Church authorized the New Testament. It is the Church who "owns" Scripture; individuals do not. And the pope plays a pivotal role in all of this, a role Pope Benedict XVI describes as "the first preserver of Christian memory, the living Church across time."

Divine revelation is always progressive in nature—that is, over time, we are granted a fuller and fuller knowledge of God in general, including a fuller understanding of the meaning of prior revelation. The New Testament did not abolish the truth of the Old Testament but extends and deepens it. Although revelation came to its fullest manifestation in Jesus, its understanding would still need further completion. According to the Gospel of John, "I have many more things to say to you, but you cannot bear them now. But when He, the Spirit of truth, comes, He will guide you into all the truth; for He will not speak on His own initiative, but whatever He hears, He will speak; and He will disclose to you what is to come" (John 16:12–13). Roy Schoeman has described this process well:

Abraham was given a fuller knowledge of God, and a greater intimacy with him, than any of his predecessors had since the Fall. Then, when God revealed himself to Moses in the burning bush, he gave Moses a yet fuller revelation of the divine Name, which had been withheld from mankind until then.... Similarly, the Messianic prophecies in the Old Testament contain veiled information about the Messiah that became clear only later, through the life of Jesus himself and through the inspiration of the Gospel writers. And so it is throughout the rest of salvation history.... Many of the central doctrines of Christianity, including the Trinitarian nature of God, the divinity of Jesus, and the perpetual virginity of Mary, only gradually became clear in the centuries following Jesus's death. (pp. 80–81)

In other words, Christianity came into the world as a single idea, but time was needed for believers to perceive its multiple aspects and to spell out its full meaning. It is for this reason that the doctrine of the faith undergoes a process of development through time. The fact that slavery is not explicitly condemned in the New Testament does not automatically make it an acceptable, morally right institution. Besides, there are many other Biblical sources that suggest that slavery is in violation with God's laws.

One of the most important doctrines in this context is that God created each one of us in his image and likeness. That's where our human dignity comes from and all our other human rights. That is why St. Isidore of Seville could say that "God has made no difference between the soul of the slave and that of the freedman." This amounts to saying that slavery is a violation of the dignity of the human person. The idea of human dignity is basically and fundamentally a Judeo-Christian concept, grounded in the fact that human beings are made in the image and likeness of God. We are subjects, not objects.

Pope John Paul II has drawn attention to the two radically different meanings of the word "my." When I say, "This is my phone," I mean I *own* the phone. On the other hand, when I say, "This is my wife," it is clear I am not claiming I own her, but I am *part* of her. That's where slavery goes wrong: it reduces subjects that we can be connected with to objects that we can own. "My co-worker" is someone I am connected with, but "my slave" is someone I pretend to own.

It is because of this that the Church should speak out against any violations of human rights and human dignity, in spite of the fact that it took many in the Church a long time to come to grips with this. But the story is not complete yet. One single event at the origin of humanity—original sin—has changed human life on earth drastically and dramatically. Since then, we are all prone to treat others as objects at our own disposal—not as subjects but objects. It is a result of original sin that our sense of morality has been corrupted—which has led to the dichotomy between values and evaluations. The Fall in Paradise shows us that Adam and Eve did not like God's commandments, because they didn't want to be commanded. They wanted to be "like God" in the sense of "next to God," but not "under God"; they wanted to be creators, not creatures; they wanted to be their own commanders-in-chief—and thereby they introduced moral evil, including slavery.

All of a sudden, with the Fall, moral evil had entered the scene. Adam and Eve could no longer treat each other as *subjects* but as objects. And the same happened in the slave trade: the other has become an object, purely at our mercy. Slavery is the condition of involuntary servitude in which a human being is regarded as no more than the property of another, as being without basic human rights—in other words, as a thing rather than a person. Under this definition, slavery is intrinsically evil, since no person may legitimately be regarded or treated as a mere thing or object, as something we own.

Slavery is a system under which people are treated as property to be bought and sold, and in which they are forced to work. It is an immoral system because it systemically and necessarily reduces its subjects to mere objects existing solely to satisfy the means of others' ends. Chattel slavery exploits humans as property. As Pope Leo XIII put it in his 1888 Encyclical *In Plurimis*:

> From the first sin came all evils, and specially this perversity that there were men who, forgetful of the original brotherhood of the race, instead of seeking, as they should naturally have done, to

promote mutual kindness and mutual respect, following their evil desires began to think of other men as their inferiors, and to hold them as cattle born for the yoke.

The Bible wants to give us back what we have lost through the Fall—that God created us in his image and likeness. Slavery is only possible because of the Fall, but this does not change the fact that slaves are creatures made in his image and likeness. Our evaluations have obscured our values. That's the awareness the Church wants to give us back—or at least should have given us back. St. Augustine worded the situation well when he said:

> No one can state satisfactorily how many fall into this same nefarious business because of the incredible blindness and greed and some kind of infection by this disease. Who would believe, for instance, that there is a woman among us here in Hippo who, as a matter of course, lures women from Gidda under the pretext of buying wood, and then confines, beats and sells them? ... A young man, scarcely twenty, an intelligent fellow, who kept the accounts for our monastery, was led astray and sold; only with the greatest difficulty was the church able to procure his freedom.

Although the Bible does not explicitly condemn slavery, it does assert, as we have seen, that the doctrine of creation does not allow human beings to hold others as cattle born for the yoke. In addition, it gives us the Ten Commandments that indirectly condemn slavery—specifically, the Seventh Commandment. The Catechism (CCC 2414) summed up Catholic teaching on slavery by citing this Commandment against stealing:

> The seventh commandment forbids acts or enterprises that for any reason—selfish or ideological, commercial, or totalitarian—lead to the enslavement of human beings, to their being bought, sold and exchanged like merchandise, in disregard for their personal dignity. It is a sin against the dignity of persons and their fundamental rights to reduce them by violence to their productive value or to a source of profit. St. Paul directed a Christian master to treat his Christian slave "no longer as a slave but more than a slave, as a beloved brother, ... both in the flesh and in the Lord."

Continuity with Change

How persistent and consistent has the Church been in condemning slavery? Some are intent on finding continuity, others on finding discontinuity in the Church's position regarding slavery. Let's rephrase the question more directly: Has the Church reversed her teaching on slavery? The anti-Catholic myths regarding slavery want us to believe that the Church has finally reversed her teaching on slavery—from completely in favor to completely opposed.

It is a common misconception that the Church did not correct its teaching on the moral legitimacy of slavery until 1965, with the publication, from the Second Vatican Council, of *Gaudium et Spes*:

> Whatever insults human dignity, such as subhuman living conditions, arbitrary imprisonment, deportation, slavery . . . the selling of women and children; as well as disgraceful working conditions, where men are treated as mere tools for profit, rather than as free and responsible persons; all these things and others of their like are infamies indeed . . . they are a supreme dishonor to the Creator.

The crucial anti-Catholic argument is this: Catholicism must be false because it once endorsed slavery, but now it does not anymore. It is easy to call such a "policy change" a case of hypocrisy, but such a verdict is not fair. As I have shown already in the previous chapters, the Church and her popes repeatedly did condemn slavery publicly and officially, at least as far back as 1435. In his 1839 Bull *In Supremo Apostulatus*, Pope Gregory XVI could cite various predecessors and their antislavery teachings; he mentions the efforts of Clement I, Pius II, Paul III, Benedict XIV, Urban VIII, and Pius VII—all of them from centuries ago. Based on such records, any earlier ambiguity about the tolerance of chattel slavery has been eradicated. Nevertheless, the Church tried very hard to grapple with the complexity of slavery. She did so during a long process of making some helpful, albeit sometimes convenient, distinctions.

First, there was the distinction between Church and State. What is allowed in the State may not be allowed in the Church. Slavery was seen as an economic, political institution. Within the Church there are no slaves, but they happen to exist outside the Church.

Perhaps a convenient distinction, but it was useful when the Church had hardly any impact on the State. As a consequence, slavery was long regarded as essentially an issue of secular law.

Second, there is the distinction between natural and positive law. Throughout Christian antiquity and the Middle Ages, theologians generally followed St. Augustine in holding that although slavery was not written into the natural moral law, it was not absolutely forbidden by that law. St. Thomas Aquinas, Martin Luther, and John Calvin were all Augustinian on this point. Although slavery— the subjection of one person to another—was not part of the primary intention of the natural law, St. Thomas taught that it was appropriate and socially useful in a world impaired by original sin. Aquinas explicitly rejected the notion that slavery is justified by *natural* law, since he held that all men are equal by nature, deducing that all "rational creatures" are entitled to justice. For Aquinas, slavery only arises through *positive* law. He held that slavery could be consistent with natural law if it is imposed by positive law as punishment for crimes, and if such slavery does not violate the slave's rights to food, sleep, marriage, raising of children, and religious worship (and anything else that pertains to natural law).

Third, there might be "degrees of evil" in slavery. At some point in time, the Catholic Church did endorse the principle that slavery could be justified as "the lesser of evils" in certain circumstances. To sell oneself for a sum and a period of time to the service of another might aid those dependents (if any) for whom one can no longer provide and give one a roof and meals to keep oneself alive. It is clear from this that, compared to bondage slavery, chattel slavery is "the worst of evils." Radical forms of slavery that deprive human beings of all personal rights are never morally permissible, but more or less moderate forms of subjection and servitude may always accompany the human condition.

Fourth, some theologians distinguished "just" from "unjust" slavery. Whether a particular slave was "justly" or "unjustly" kept in that condition could depend on his or her religious status. The Church long accepted the right of people to sell themselves or their children into slavery or to be sentenced to slavery as a criminal punishment. In other words, slavery was considered "just," firstly, when it proceeded from a legitimate war or voluntary sale; secondly, provided it respected the soul, body, family, and instruction of the slave. Since "just" slavery had been allowed by previous Councils and popes, the declaration of all kinds of slavery as an unconditional "infamy" in the Second Vatican Council pastoral constitution *Gaudium et Spes* was a correction to what had been previously allowed, but was never promulgated as infallible teaching.

Fifth, there is the distinction between serfdom and slavery. Serfdom did not involve the humiliation and brutality people today ordinarily associate with slavery. Moral theologians recognized that slaves, unlike mere chattels, had certain rights even against their masters, who no longer had over them the power of life and death, as had been the case in pagan antiquity. However, there are circumstances in which a person can be justly compelled to servitude against his will. Prisoners of war or criminals, for example, can justly lose their circumstantial freedom and be forced into servitude, within certain limits. Moreover, people can also "sell" their labor for a period of time. The just titles to servitude were not rejected by the Church, but rather were tolerated for many reasons. Even nowadays we consider imprisonment "just" under certain circumstances.

Sixth, we could distinguish slavery from slave-trading. The Church may not always have been explicitly against slavery as such, but she did raise her voice repeatedly against slave-trading. Speaking at the infamous "House of Slaves" on the Island of Gorée in Senegal, from which innumerable slaves had been exported, Pope John Paul II declared in 1992: "It is fitting to confess in all truth and humility this sin of man against man, this sin of man against God." Given the context of his speech, the pope is here speaking of the slave trade, which had repeatedly been condemned. Far from changing the doctrine, John Paul was here explicitly reaffirming the position of Pope Pius II, whom he quoted as having declared in 1492 that the slave trade was an immense crime.

When Pope Gregory XVI in his 1839 Bull *In Supremo Apostolatus* condemned slavery, it was misread by many as condemning only slave-trade. Even Bishop John England of Charleston in South Carolina misinterpreted the Bull and noted that the Pontiff was condemning only the slave trade and not slavery itself, especially as it existed in the United States. However, it is hard to deny that Gregory wrote *In Supremo* to condemn precisely what was occurring in the United States, namely the enslavement of blacks:

> We, by apostolic authority, warn and strongly exhort in the Lord faithful Christians of every condition that no one in the future dare to bother unjustly, despoil of their possessions, or reduce to slavery Indians, Blacks or other such peoples.

However, since Pope Gregory XVI admonished and adjured "all believers in Christ, of whatsoever condition, that no one hereafter may dare *unjustly* to molest Indians, Blacks, or other men of this sort; . . . or to reduce them to slavery," Catholic bishops in the American South focused on the word "unjustly." They argued that the Pope did not condemn slavery if the slaves had been captured *justly*—that is, they were either criminals or prisoners of war. Hence, the bishops determined that this prohibition did not apply to slavery in the United States. But the slavery of the colonial period was very different from slavery during biblical times. As a matter of fact, it exploited and enslaved people who had no debt, had committed no crimes, and had not waged war.

Were all the above distinctions just terminological hairsplitting maneuverings? Or were they necessary steps to gradually come to grips with the complexity of the slavery issue under constantly changing circumstances? The former is a cynical, and altogether too technical way of viewing the matter; the latter, though, places it in a more intelligible and helpful framework. For the Church does not perform a reversal of her original teaching, but rather adds nuances to it. In view of a changing societal system, the Church clarified rather than overturned her previous teaching. We could even speak here in terms of "reform," which is more akin to "renewal" than simple "change."

Changes in the Church follow a different course in social ethics than in the realm of doctrine. The formulation of revealed truth develops through the discernment of new truths that are formally implicit in the apostolic deposit. This process of growth resembles the way a river growths—it gets wider and deeper, while remaining the same river. Such truths, once proclaimed by the Church as divinely revealed, are dogmas and must be held by all as matters of divine and Catholic faith. They determine the correct interpretation of the Scriptures. As the late, great Dorothy Sayers said, the drama is in the dogma, for which our ancestors were willing to die. Hence, the Church cannot deny in one age what she has affirmed in a previous age as essential dogma.

Social teaching, though, as the late Cardinal Avery Dulles, S.J., has pointed out, is different from doctrinal development. Social teaching consists of behavioral norms for social conduct in conformity with the Gospel. While the principles remain constant, the proximate norms are not free from contingency because society itself is in flux. Specific regulations rarely have the universal and permanent character that belongs to dogma. Development in social teaching is not simply a matter of articulating what was always implicitly taught, but rather a way of applying the teaching to new social situations.

Pope John Paul II noted the interplay of continuity and change in several of his social encyclicals. In the 1987 *Sollicitudo Rei Socialis*, for example, he declared that the Church's teaching in the social sphere exhibits both permanence and constant renewal:

> On the one hand it is constant, for it remains identical in its fundamental inspiration, in its "principles of reflection," in its "criteria of judgment," in its basic "directives for action," and above all in its vital link with the Gospel of the Lord. On the other hand, it is ever new, because it is subject to the necessary and opportune adaptations suggested by the changes in historical conditions and by the unceasing flow of the events which are the setting of the life of people and society.

The Pontiff explains here that the social teaching of the Magisterium is under continual revision insofar as the unchanging principles of the gospel need to be upheld in changing social situations. The fundamental principles are constant, but the judgments and adaptations are ever new. This would also apply to the issue of slavery—a social teaching issue par excellence. Circumstances may change, but the principles remain the same. The Church changed its moral teaching on slavery, not to suit the times, but to acknowledge the times. For instance, in his meeting with seventeen newly appointed ambassadors to the Holy See, Pope Francis I encouraged them to work together, regardless of creed, against the "slavery" of human trafficking—a very recent offshoot of slavery. Times may change but the principles should not.

Myth 2
Crusades, Catholic Aggression

T he general view is that the crusades were a series of military expeditions organized by the Christian powers of Western Europe against the Muslim powers who ruled the traditional Holy Land of Christianity.

The hidden message is clear: The crusaders were the aggressors and the Muslims were merely victims who had to defend themselves. How much of this is truth, and how much has been colored by anti-Christian bias? First of all, there is no denying that Christians and Muslims have different views of violence and aggression. When Christians use violence in wars and so on, they are not following the Gospel, nor the example of Christ. When Muslims are using it, they are following the Koran and Mohammed's example.

Second, it was anti-Catholic propaganda that invented the name "crusade," just as it invented the term "Dark Ages"; they were chosen by "enlightened" historians to describe the deviation of darkness and fanaticism between the splendors of antiquity and the Renaissance. The French form of the word *crusade* first appears in the *L'Histoire des Croisades* written by A. de Clermont and published in 1638.

Third, those who joined the crusades had no idea they were in a crusade. They were known by various terms, including *fideles Sancti Petri* (the faithful of Saint Peter) or *milites Christi* (knights of Christ)—but never crusaders. The origin of the word crusader may be traced to the cross (*crux*) made of cloth and worn as a badge on the outer garment of those who took part in these enterprises. This "taking of the cross" eventually became associated with the entire journey.

In other words, the crusaders saw themselves as undertaking a journey, a peregrination. It is essential to understand that the crusades were actually penitential pilgrimages. "Taking the cross" meant taking a vow. But high ideals may not always guarantee a good outcome.

The History of the Crusades

The Bare Facts

In 1095, an assembly of churchmen called by Pope Urban II met at Clermont, France. Messengers from the Byzantine Emperor Alexius I had urged the pope to send help against the armies of Muslim Turks. By the end of the 12th century, the Muslim Turks had turned their attention to the Near East. The conquering Muslim hordes swept through the Christian East, and finally turned toward Constantinople. The new Emperor, Alexius, realized his weakened state and appealed to Western Christendom for help to protect his crumbling empire.

On November 27, Pope Urban addressed the assembly and asked the warriors of Europe to liberate the Holy Land from the Muslims. The response of the assembly was overwhelmingly favorable. While figures vary, it is estimated that from 60,000 to 100,000 Europeans were inspired to "take up the cross" and begin the expedition of what was later called the First Crusade. Soon Europe was on the march toward Jerusalem.

Thus was launched the first and most successful of at least eight crusades against the Muslim caliphates of the Near East. The Crusaders, known to the Muslims as the *Franj* or *Franks*, reached Jerusalem on Tuesday, June 7, 1099, and began their siege. Finally, by the end of the first decade of the 12th century, they were able to establish crusader states, also called Latin Kingdoms, at Edessa, Antioch, Tripoli, and Jerusalem.

Subsequent efforts to maintain these states met with various degrees of success. The next two centuries saw seven more major expeditions. The Second Crusade, 1147–49, headed by King Louis VII, was called for by various preachers, most notably by St. Bernard of Clairvaux, at the request of Pope Eugenius III, who had been one of his monks at Clairvaux. But that Crusade turned out to be a disastrous failure. It ended in a Muslim triumph, sparked by the fall of Edessa in 1144. Roundly criticized for its failure, St. Bernard said that he had launched it for a divine cause and that the sins of the armies had ruined it.

Apparently, the Muslims had been able to regroup themselves. They had long fought among themselves, but they were finally united by Saladin, who created a single powerful state. Following his victory at the Battle of Hattin, Saladin easily overwhelmed the disunited crusaders in 1187 and retook Jerusalem on September 29, 1187. Terms were arranged and the city surrendered, with Saladin entering the city on 2 October 1187.

Saladin was the greatest warrior of the Muslims. He also proved to be a skilled diplomat. The Muslim world was divided into the Shiite and Sunni religious sects, as well as the warring secular nations of the Syrians, Egyptians, and Turks. Saladin was the one who brought all of them into one unified Islamic force in the 12th century. Not surprisingly, Saladin's victories shocked Europe. On hearing news of the Siege of Jerusalem (1187), Pope Urban III died of a heart attack on October 19, 1187. On 29 October, Pope Gregory VIII issued a papal bull *Audita Tremendi*, calling for the Third Crusade; he died on 17 December 1187 of a fever after holding the papacy for only 57 days.

The Third Crusade, 1188–92, was conducted by Emperor Frederick Barbarossa, King Philip Augustus of France, and King Richard "Lion-Heart" of England. During the Third Crusade, King Richard captured Cyprus and Acre, but failed to recapture the city of Jerusalem. Richard went back to England the following year after negotiating a treaty with Saladin. The treaty allowed trade for merchants and unarmed Christian pilgrims to make pilgrimages to Jerusalem, while it remained under Muslim control.

The Fourth Crusade, 1202–1204, was initiated by Pope Innocent III in 1200 with preaching taking place in France, England, and Germany, although the bulk of the efforts were in France. The crusade was to be directed at Egypt, because the Crusaders believed that conquering it would be the key to regaining Jerusalem. The conquering of the great Christian city in 1204 ended the Fourth Crusade and had significant religious and political consequences. This crusade remained notorious for the sacking of Constantinople in

1203—an event that earned the permanent enmity of the Greek Byzantine Church (more on this later).

The Fifth Crusade, 1217–1221, was called by Pope Innocent III, along with his summoning of the Fourth Lateran Council in 1215. The majority of the crusaders came from Germany, Flanders, and Frisia, along with a large army from Hungary led by King Andrew II, and other forces led by Duke Leopold VI. The forces of Andrew and Leopold arrived in Acre in October 1217 but little was accomplished, and Andrew returned to Hungary in January 1218. After the arrival of more crusaders, Leopold and the king of Jerusalem, John of Brienne, laid siege to Damietta in Egypt, which they captured finally in November 1219. Blocked by forces of Sultan Al-Kamil, the crusaders were forced to surrender. The Sultan forced the return of Damietta and agreed to an eight-year truce while the crusaders left Egypt.

The Sixth Crusade, 1228–29, was connected to Emperor Frederick II. He had repeatedly vowed a crusade but failed to live up to his words, for which he was excommunicated by Gregory IX in 1228. He finally set sail from Brindisi in June 1228 and landed at Acre in September 1228. There were no battles as Frederick made a peace treaty with Al-Kamil, the ruler of Egypt. This treaty allowed Christians to rule over most of Jerusalem and a strip of territory from Acre to Jerusalem, while the Muslims were given control of their sacred areas in Jerusalem. In return, Frederick pledged to protect Al-Kamil against all his enemies, even if they were Christian.

The Seventh Crusade, 1248–54, was not started by a pope, but by King Louis IX of France, who later became known as St. Louis. He was the only man interested in beginning another crusade when Jerusalem was taken by Muslims again in 1244. The fall of Jerusalem was no longer an earth-shattering event to European Christians, who had seen the city pass from Christian to Muslim control numerous times over the past two centuries. This time, despite calls from the pope, there was no popular enthusiasm for a new crusade, until Louis took up the case. Egypt was the object of his crusade, and he landed in 1249 at Damietta on the Nile. Egypt, Louis thought, would provide a base from which to attack Jerusalem, and its wealth and supply of grain would keep the crusaders fed and equipped. But in 1254 Louis ran out of money, and his presence was needed in France where his mother had recently died. Before leaving, he established a standing French garrison at Acre, the capital of the Kingdom of Jerusalem after the loss of Jerusalem, at the expense of the French crown; it remained there until the fall of Acre in 1291.

The enthusiasm for the crusades, already dying in the 13th century, totally subsided after the fall of Tripoli and Acre in 1289–91. The lack of a unified command was only one of the reasons why, from a purely worldly standpoint, the crusades seemed unlikely of success.

The Original Motives

Misconceptions about the crusades are all too common. They are seen by many as the epitome of self-righteousness and intolerance, a black stain on the history of the Catholic Church in particular and Western civilization in general.

Is this a fair assessment of the crusade history? Let me explain why I am convinced it is not. When Pope Urban II called for the First Crusade, he stressed three important reasons for his plea: (1) the molestation of pilgrims in the Holy Land; (2) the desecration of holy Christian places; and (3) the plight of Eastern Christians in distress. In 1095, when the Pontiff proclaimed the first crusade, his main goal was to restore Christian access to the holy places in and near Jerusalem. Because pilgrimages to the Holy Land were very popular at the time, it was no surprise that the disruption of pilgrimages by conquering Seljuk Turks prompted strong support for the crusades in Western Europe.

Let me stress what was *not* a motive for the crusades. It is often assumed that the central goal of the crusades was forced conversion of the Muslim world. Nothing could be further from the truth. Muslims who lived in crusader-won territories were generally allowed to retain their property and livelihood, and always their religion. As a matter of fact, throughout the history of the Crusader Kingdom of Jerusalem, Muslim inhabitants far outnumbered the Catholics. It was not until the 13th century that the Franciscans began conversion efforts among Muslims. But these were mostly unsuccessful and finally abandoned.

Neither was greed, driven by poverty, a motive. As the historian Thomas Madden has remarked, "it was not those with the least to lose who took up the cross, but rather those with the most." Instead, the reaction was instigated by pure enthusiasm. The overwhelming response to Pope Urban's speech must have startled even the pope. Large numbers of Franks, both noble and common, answered his call with great enthusiasm and streamed eastward in several waves. It was not greed but religious fervor that incited them—if only for the simple reason that crusading was a hard, lonely, expensive, dangerous proposition. But because large numbers of poorer knights and peasants also answered the call immediately and set off without proper preparation, this sort of participation was not what the authorities had had in mind, and no one was prepared to deal with the dire consequences.

But what about the pope's main reasons—the molestation of pilgrims in the Holy Land, the desecration of holy Christian places, and the plight of Eastern Christians in distress? To understand his reasons, we need to delve more deeply into the history of Jerusalem.

Even though crusading efforts were not directed exclusively to Jerusalem, the Holy City was always the core, the very heart of the crusades. The goal of Jerusalem was what made the crusade a pilgrimage. As the ground made holy by the passion, death, and resurrection of Christ, Jerusalem was the most sacred site of pilgrimage for Christians from the earliest centuries on. From the time of Christ up until the conversion of Constantine in 312, Jerusalem had been in pagan hands. With the emperor's conversion, Jerusalem became a Christian city and was thereupon adorned with great shrines and churches commemorating all aspects of Christ's final days, the most glorious edifice being the great Church of the Holy Sepulcher. For Christians, the Church of the Holy Sepulcher in Jerusalem commemorated the hill of crucifixion and the tomb of Christ's burial. No wonder Jerusalem was a favorite goal for many a pilgrimage. In short, the City of Jerusalem held a holy significance to the Christian religion.

This was only possible as long as Jerusalem would remain in Christian hands, which lasted until 614. At that time, Zoroastrian Persians under Khosrau II invaded the Holy City. They slaughtered tens of thousands of inhabitants, and sold the survivors into slavery. In 630, the Christian Byzantine emperor Heraclius recovered Jerusalem, but Muslims took the Holy City again in 638. Even though pilgrimage routes to the Holy Land remained open for a while, Muslims controlled the most important site of Christian pilgrimage.

By the 8th century, Islamic forces had conquered North Africa, the eastern shores of the Mediterranean, and most of Spain. Islamic armies established bases in Italy, greatly reduced the size and power of the Byzantine Empire (the Eastern Roman Empire) and besieged its capital, Constantinople. The Byzantine Empire, which had preserved much of the classical civilization of the Greeks and had defended the eastern Mediterranean from assaults from all sides, was barely able to hold off the enemy.

Pilgrimages were not cut off at first, but after Jerusalem was taken by the caliph Umar early in the 11th century the Fatimid caliph Hakim began to persecute the Christians and despoiled the Holy Sepulcher. Persecution abated after his death (1021), but relations remained strained and became more so when Jerusalem passed, in 1071, from the comparatively tolerant Egyptians to the Seljuk Turks, who in the same year defeated the Byzantine emperor Romanus IV at Manzikert. The Holy City was in real danger.

It was during the first century of the second millennium that things came to a head. In 1010, the Muslim caliph al-Hakim had already ordered the destruction of all Christian shrines and churches. The arrival of the Seljuk Turks (non-Arab Muslims), who conquered Jerusalem from the Egyptian Muslims in the late 11th century, negatively altered the landscape for the Christians. In 1065, the Seljuks began a campaign of persecution against Christian pilgrims in the Holy Land. During this campaign, the bishop of Bamberg, for instance, and 12,000 pilgrims were massacred by the Muslims only two miles from Jerusalem. In 1071, the Muslim Seljuk Turks defeated the Christian Byzantine forces and cut off the pilgrimage routes, thus setting the stage for the announcement of the First Crusade.

As to why the First Crusade started, historians mention a series of reasons—ranging from political to economic to religious elements. I leave them for what they are worth. But it is hard to deny that the massive positive reaction Pope Urban received in response to his call was only possible because the individual participants of the crusades felt a strong *religious* drive to respond. It is difficult to believe that the Crusade could have succeeded without an extraordinary dedication to the ultimate objective, the liberation of the Holy City of Jerusalem. Crusaders were supposed to take a *Crusade Vow*—a promise made to God by a pious Christian that he would journey to the Holy Sepulcher in Jerusalem in the ranks of an organized and armed expedition approved by the papacy. "Taking the cross"—as a badge on their outer garment—meant taking a vow, which was made in public, before witnesses, and was binding in the eyes of God and the Church.

After the astonishing success of the First Crusade, many crusaders fulfilled their vows by completing their pilgrimage at the Church of the Holy Sepulcher and went back home. Others stayed, however, and continued to build up a new society. One of their contributions to history was the formation of knightly orders such as the Knights Templar, the Teutonic Knights, and the Hospitallers. These were orders of religious knights, working from monastic rule to defend the Holy Land and pilgrims en route to Jerusalem. The members of these orders were both monks and knights; that is, to the monastic vows of chastity, poverty, and obedience, they added a fourth vow, which bound them to protect pilgrims. In other words, these orders were both a response to the desperate need for manpower in the East, and an example of the way the Church was attempting to tame and even monasticize the warrior class.

The spiritual zeal prompted by Pope Urban II helped to inspire the remarkable outcome of the First Crusade. The goal to recapture Jerusalem, to aid the Byzantine East, and to unite Europe in a common cause was a noble effort. Although the crusades in essence proved to be an example of a high-minded ideal, they were also often betrayed by human nature. Subsequent crusades, in the hands of warring noblemen, knights, and clerics who often struggled for power, land, and riches, proved disastrous, particularly with the Fourth Crusade.

How has later history assessed the crusades? During the Reformation and Counter-Reformation of the 16th century, historians saw the crusades through the prism of their own religious beliefs. Protestants saw them as a manifestation of the evils of the papacy, whereas Catholics viewed the movement as a force for good. Martin Luther was the first within Christianity who argued in a very forcible way that to fight in the crusades as a Christian would be the same as fighting Christ Himself. He believed that Christ had sent the Turks to punish the Catholic Church for its infidelity to God.

But none of this can alter the fact that Pope Urban II, in a speech at Clermont in France in November 1095, called for a great Christian expedition to free Jerusalem from the Seljuk Turks, a new Muslim power that had recently begun actively harassing peaceful Christian pilgrims traveling to Jerusalem. The pope was spurred by his position as the spiritual head of Western Europe as well as by a call for help from the Byzantine emperor, Alexius I. These various factors were genuine causes, and, at the same time, useful justifications for the Pope's call for a crusade. In any case, Pope Urban's speech appealed to thousands of people of all classes. It was the right message at the right time:

> The noble race of Franks must come to aid their fellow Christians in the East. The infidel Turks are advancing into the heart of Eastern Christendom; Christians are being oppressed and attacked; churches and holy places are being defiled. Jerusalem is groaning under the Saracen yoke. The Holy Sepulcher is in Moslem hands and has been turned into a mosque. Pilgrims are harassed and even prevented from access to the Holy Land.
>
> The West must march to the defense of the East. All should go, rich and poor alike. The Franks must stop their internal wars and squabbles. Let them go instead against the infidel and fight a righteous war.

Where Did Things Go Wrong?

What Went Wrong?

Did things go wrong during the crusades? They certainly, and unfortunately, did. The original motives behind the crusades may have been sincere and deeply spiritual, but military and political aspirations soon interfered. In fact, the conflict between spiritual and material aims became increasingly upsetting.

The main problem during each crusade was that there was no

unified command. True, it was always popes that proclaimed the crusades, but they had great difficulty controlling the crusaders, and besides, they were not "on the field." Those who were on the field were not under a unified command, and those whom we consider "leaders" of each crusade often acted independently or even against each other.

As a consequence, some groups of crusaders acted on their own—sometimes completely out of control—which led occasionally to atrocious killings. Their emotions often overruled their original motives. A majority of those who took the vow for the crusades were deeply motivated by their love of Christ; and undeniably, religious fervor was a main source of inspiration throughout the crusade. However, the greed for earthly riches, the petty rivalries of the leaders, and the brutality of war—among other motives—would soon create troubles for the crusaders far beyond their own control.

When the French crusaders on their way to Jerusalem crossed into Germany in the spring of 1096, for example, units of crusaders massacred hundreds or thousands of Jews in the cities of Speyer, Worms, Mainz, and Cologne, despite efforts by Catholic bishops to protect the Jews. Fifty years later, when the Second Crusade was gearing up, St. Bernard of Clairvaux had to frequently preach that the Jews were not to be persecuted:

> Ask anyone who knows the Sacred Scriptures what he finds foretold of the Jews in the Psalm. "Not for their destruction do I pray," it says. The Jews are for us the living words of Scripture, for they remind us always of what our Lord suffered. . . . Under Christian princes they endure a hard captivity, but "they only wait for the time of their deliverance."

Although the First Crusade was the most successful from a military point of view, accounts of its actions are shocking. For example, the contemporary chronicler Raymond of Agiles described the capture of Jerusalem by the Crusaders in 1099:

> Some of our men cut off the heads of their enemies; others shot them with arrows, so that they fell from the towers; others tortured them longer by casting them into the flames. Piles of heads, hands and feet were to be seen in the streets of the city. It was nec-

essary to pick one's way over the bodies of men and horses. But these were small matters compared to what happened at the temple of Solomon, a place where religious services ware ordinarily chanted. What happened there? If I tell the truth, it will exceed your powers of belief. So let it suffice to say this much at least, that in the temple and portico of Solomon, men rode in blood up to their knees and bridle reins.

The crusader armies initially fought the Turks at the lengthy Siege of Antioch that began in October 1097 and lasted until June 1098. Once inside the city, the crusaders massacred the Muslim inhabitants and pillaged the city. Jews and Muslims fought together to defend Jerusalem against the invading Franks. On July 15, 1099, when the crusaders entered the city, they proceeded to massacre the remaining Jewish and Muslim civilians and looted or destroyed mosques and the city itself. That was a crusade gone astray, in spite of its military success.

A second problem of the crusades was that, although the crusade was originally a "pilgrimage" to Jerusalem, it took on the cloak of a "holy war." And wars come with costs. Besides, they are seen as un-Christian. The Ten Commandments tell us, "Thou shalt not kill." Jesus Christ was an advocate of peace. St. Martin of Tours in the fourth century declared "I am a soldier of Christ; I must not fight." So how could popes justify a war when Christianity was a religion of peace?

From its very beginning, Christianity had an ambivalent attitude towards warfare. Although there was always a pacifist faction within Christianity, pacifism was never the official position of the Church. In fact, some of the first Christian converts were soldiers and apparently remained at their jobs after their conversion (see Acts 10). After the Roman government became officially Christian, however, Christian officials needed guidelines for the use of violence. In response to this need, the doctrine of Just War was developed. It assumed that violence was evil, but acknowledged that passivity in the face of others' violence might be a greater evil—this was waging war only to build peace.

St. Augustine held that war was just at the bidding of God or a legitimate authority with the proper intention and for a right cause—such as defense of one's life and property or recovering lost territory. Once Church and State became more and more closely intertwined, some thinkers concluded that this meant that Christ's Will for mankind, embodied in the Church, could still be advanced by the political structures of Christian peoples. They also argued that violence might not simply be the "lesser of two evils" (as the doctrine of Just War stipulated); violence, they said, was morally neutral, and those who used violence to advance Christ's kingdom might be doing positive good. The doctrine of Just War was yielding to the doctrine known as *Holy War.*

Then there was another change occurring at the time of the crusades—the rise of the nobility (the warrior classes) of the West. Fighting men had defended Christian civilization against successive waves of barbarian assaults (including Vikings, Magyars, and others) during the second half of the first millennium, but by the eleventh century the barbarians were either tamed or destroyed. Only the Muslims, also known as Saracens, were left as potential targets for these warriors.

Because it was a war, atrocities occurred on both sides. We mentioned already the massacres caused by Christians. But the other side committed its own atrocities: with the fall of Tripoli in 1289 and Acre in 1291, for instance, those Christians unable to leave the cities were massacred or enslaved. Although there were atrocities on both sides, there were also real heroes on both sides. Two figures that received lasting respect by both Christian and Muslim historians alike were Saladin and St. Francis of Assisi. In fact, both were immortalized in a favorable light by Dante in his Divine Comedy. It was St. Francis who accompanied the crusaders to Egypt on the Fifth Crusade, and boldly walked right into the Muslim camp of al-Malik al-Kamil, nephew of the great Saladin who had defeated the forces of the hapless Third Crusade. Francis was admitted to the sultan himself and spoke to him of Christ, who was, after all, Francis's only subject. Trying to proselytize a Muslim would be cause for on-the-spot decapitation, but Kamil was deeply impressed by Francis courage and sincerity and invited him to stay for a week of serious conversation. Francis, in turn, was deeply impressed by the religious devotion of the sultan. Some call it a tragedy of history that Kamil and Francis were unable to talk longer. Had they been able to do so, the phrase "clash of civilizations" might be unknown to our world.

Another Detrimental Incident

Since the Enlightenment, historians have criticized the crusading movement in many ways. The most common accusation is that Christian powers and Muslim powers were attacking each other. But, more in particular, some historians have pointed to the Fourth Crusade which, instead of attacking Islam, attacked another Christian power—the Eastern Roman Empire. This was seen by many as a nefarious "betrayal" of Byzantium.

How could this dramatic turn of events take place? The Fourth Crusade (1202–1204) was originally intended to conquer Muslim-controlled Jerusalem by means of an invasion through Egypt. Instead, in April 1204, the crusaders of Western Europe invaded and sacked the Orthodox Christian city of Constantinople, capital of the Byzantine Empire. What had changed their course? The story is quite intricate and bizarre.

Pope Innocent III had succeeded to the papacy in January 1198, and the preaching of a new crusade became the prime goal of his pontificate. His call was largely ignored by the European monarchs, but a crusading army was finally organized under the leadership of an Italian count, Boniface of Montferrat. Boniface and the other leaders sent envoys to Venice, Genoa, and other city-states in 1200 to negotiate a contract for transport to Egypt, the object of their crusade. The crusading army was expected to consist of 4,500 knights (as well as 4,500 horses), 9,000 squires, and 20,000 foot-soldiers. In March 1201, negotiations were opened with Venice which agreed to transport 33,500 crusaders—a very ambitious number. This agreement required a full year of preparation on the part of the Venetians to build numerous ships and train the sailors who would man them, all the while curtailing the city's commercial activities.

By May 1202, the bulk of the crusader army was collected at Venice, although with far smaller numbers than expected—about 12,000 instead of 33,500. The Venetians had performed their part of the agreement: There lay 50 war galleys and 450 transports—enough for three times the assembled army. However, the Venetians would not let the crusaders leave without paying the full amount agreed to, originally 85,000 silver marks. The crusaders could only pay 35,000 silver marks to start with. Doge Dandolo, who had joined the crusade, proposed that the crusaders pay their debts by intimidating many of the local ports and towns down the Adriatic Sea, culminating in an attack on the port of Zara in Dalmatia.

Many of the crusaders were opposed to attacking Zara, and some refused to participate altogether and returned home. While the papal legate to the Crusade endorsed the move as necessary to prevent the crusade's complete failure for financial reasons, the pope himself was alarmed at this development and wrote a letter to the crusading leadership threatening excommunication. In 1202, Pope Innocent III forbade the crusaders of Western Christendom from committing any atrocities against their Christian neighbors:

> For you, who ought to have looked for help for the Holy Land, you who should have stirred up others, both by word and by example, to assist the Holy Land—on your own initiative you sailed to Greece, bringing in your footsteps riot only the pilgrims, but even the natives of the Holy Land who came to Constantinople, following our venerable brother, the Archbishop of Tyre. . . . It was your duty to attend to the business of your legation and to give careful consideration, not to the capture of the Empire of Constantinople, but rather to the defense of what is left of the Holy Land and, with the Lord's leave, the restoration of what has been lost. We made you our representative and we sent you to gain, not temporal, but rather eternal riches.

Strangely enough, this letter was concealed from the bulk of the army who arrived at Zara on November 10–11, 1202, and the attack proceeded. When Pope Innocent III heard of the sack, he sent a letter to the crusaders threatening them with general and particular excommunication if they should dare to act against any Christians whatsoever; he ordered them to return to their holy vows and head for Jerusalem. Out of fear that this would dissolve the army, the leaders of the crusade decided not to inform their followers of the pope's letter. So the crusaders, desperate from want of money and sick of delay and uncertainty, accepted the Venetian terms: and on October 8, 1202, they sailed blindly into excommunication.

In the meantime, the Byzantine prince Alexios IV had offered to pay the entire debt owed to the Venetians—provided they would sail to Byzantium and topple the reigning emperor Alexios III. Doge Dandolo and Count Boniface agreed to the plan. The main objective of the crusaders was to place Alexios IV on the Byzantine throne so that they could receive the rich payments he had promised them. To take Byzantium by force, the crusaders first needed to cross the Bosporus, where Alexios III had lined up the Byzantine army in battle formation along the shore. From then on, the battle grew uglier by the moment. The crusaders eventually inflicted a savage sacking on Constantinople for three days, during which many ancient Greco-Roman and medieval Byzantine works of art were either stolen or destroyed.

Despite their oaths and the threat of excommunication by the pope, the crusaders ruthlessly and systematically violated the city's churches and monasteries, destroying, defiling, or stealing all they could lay their hands on. It is said that the total amount looted from Constantinople was about 900,000 silver marks. The Venetians received 150,000 silver marks, which was their due, while the crusaders received 50,000 silver marks. A further 100,000 silver marks were divided evenly up between the crusaders and Venetians. The remaining 500,000 silver marks were secretly kept back by many crusader knights.

The legacy of the Fourth Crusade was the deep sense of betrayal felt by the Greek Christians. This is seen as one of the final acts in the Great Schism between the Eastern Orthodox Church and the Roman Catholic Church. With the events of 1204, the schism between the Church in the West and East was not just complete but also solidified. It was also a key turning point in the decline of the empire and of Christianity in the Near East. Crippled by the Fourth Crusade, the Byzantine Empire would soon be an easy target for the Ottoman Turks who captured the city in 1453.

As an epilogue to the event, Pope Innocent III, the man who had unintentionally launched the ill-fated expedition, spoke against the crusaders with these words:

How, indeed, will the church of the Greeks, no matter how severely she is beset with afflictions and persecutions, return into ecclesiastical union and to a devotion for the Apostolic See, when she has seen in the Latins only an example of perdition and the works of darkness, so that she now, and with reason, detests the Latins more than dogs? As for those who were supposed to be seeking the ends of Jesus Christ, not their own ends, who made their swords, which they were supposed to use against the pagans, drip with Christian blood, they have spared neither religion, nor age, nor sex. They have committed incest, adultery, and fornication before the eyes of men.

Eight hundred years after the Fourth Crusade, Pope John Paul II twice expressed sorrow for the events of the Fourth Crusade. In 2001, he wrote to Christodoulos, Archbishop of Athens, saying, "It is tragic that the assailants, who set out to secure free access for Christians to the Holy Land, turned against their brothers in the faith. The fact that they were Latin Christians fills Catholics with deep regret." In 2004, while Bartholomew I, Patriarch of Constantinople, was visiting the Vatican, John Paul II asked, "How can we not share, at a distance of eight centuries, the pain and disgust?" This has been regarded as an apology to the Greek Orthodox Church for the terrible slaughter perpetrated by the warriors of the Fourth Crusade.

In April 2004, in a speech on the 800th anniversary of the city's capture, Ecumenical Patriarch Bartholomew I formally accepted the apology. "The spirit of reconciliation is stronger than hatred," he said during a liturgy attended by Roman Catholic Archbishop Philippe Barbarin of Lyon, France. "We receive with gratitude and respect your cordial gesture for the tragic events of the Fourth Crusade. It is a fact that a crime was committed here in the city 800 years ago."

In recent years, a powerful social movement has demanded that the West, and specifically the Church, apologize not only for the Fourth Crusade but also for the entire medieval crusading movement. Underlying the movement for apology, though, is the assumption that religious frontiers are somehow carved in stone, and that Muslim states of the Near East must always and infallibly have been destined to be part of the world of Islam. In contrast, an equally good case can be made that the medieval Middle East was no more inevitably Muslim than other regions conquered by Islam and subsequently liberated, like Spain and Hungary. Nor, curiously, do Westerners suggest that Muslims apologize for the aggressive acts that gave them power over those various lands in the first place.

So what is our final assessment? Viewed in the light of their original purpose, the crusades were failures. They made no permanent conquests of the Holy Land. They did not retard the advance of Islam. Far from aiding the Eastern Empire, they hastened its disintegration. They also revealed the continuing inability of Latin Christians to understand Greek Christians, and they hardened the schism between them. In addition, they were marked, and marred, by a recurrence of anti-Semitism.

As with all great human endeavors, the crusades had their high points and their low points. As T. S. Eliot has written,

> Among were a few good men,
> Many who were evil,
> And most who were neither,
> Like all men in all places.
> Those who would defend them blindly, and those who would seek to apologize for them without any question, are equally misguided.

A War between Muslims and Christians

Who Are the Aggressors?

Those who consider the crusades only in military terms like to pose the question of who were the aggressors in this series of wars and who were the victims. The crusades can be looked at from two different perspectives, of course—the Christian and the Islamic perspective. Different perspectives give us different views. After the movie *How the West Was Won*, there was a need for another movie: *How the West Was Lost*. There are usually at least two sides to any story.

Many people may think the present violence of fundamentalist Muslims has its roots in the crusades' brutal and unprovoked attacks against a sophisticated and tolerant Muslim world and that the crusaders were really the aggressors in the conflict. Osama bin Laden was certainly one who thought so. In his various video performances, he never failed to describe the American war against terrorism as a new crusade against Islam. Former president of the United States Bill Clinton has also pointed to the crusades as the root cause of the present conflict.

But who really were the aggressors? In the context of more than a thousand years of Christian-Islamic interactions, there is much evidence to claim that the Muslims had been aggressors against the Christians since the seventh century. The warriors of Islam struck out against the Christians shortly after Mohammed's death. They were extremely successful in doing so. Palestine, Syria, and Egypt—once the most heavily Christian areas in the world—quickly succumbed. When Caliph Omar conquered Jerusalem in 638, the city had been Christian for over three centuries. Soon after, the Prophet's disciples invaded and destroyed the glorious churches of North Africa, causing the extinction of Christianity in places that had boasted bishops like St. Augustine. The Church of the Resurrection in Jerusalem was burned down under the Abbasid rule in 936. Then it was dismantled, including the digging up of its foundations, by Caliph Hakim bi-Amr Allah (996–1021).

So we have a long, protracted story here of Muslim invasion and occupation. Imperialism is certainly not a Western invention; Muslims see it as the normal exercise of power. Here are some milestones of Muslim invasion: Syria (636), and the surrounding lands, all Christian—including Palestine and Iraq (636), Iraq (637), Jerusalem (638), Iran (638–650), Egypt (639–642), North Africa (643–707), Cyprus and Tripoli (644–650). Soon followed the lower Indus Valley (710–713) and Spain (711–718). The Muslim invasion of France was stopped at the Battle of Tours (also known as the Battle of Poitiers) in 732. The Franks, under their leader Charles Martel (the grandfather of Charlemagne), defeated the Muslims and turned them back out of France. But the sequence of Muslim occupations did not end here.

In the eleventh century, the Seljuk Turks conquered Asia Minor, which had been Christian since the time of St. Paul. In 1071 the Turks attacked and virtually annihilated the Byzantine army at

Manzikert. No wonder, in his desperation, the emperor in Constantinople sent word to the Christians of Western Europe asking them to aid their brothers and sisters in the East. The Mediterranean had become a "Muslim Lake." So by looking back at all of the Muslim attacks on Christian civilization for more than four centuries before the first Crusade in 1095, it is apparent that the Catholic Church had actually been very patient in fighting back against assaults by the Muslim Turk aggressors. But her patience began to wear thin.

At this juncture the crusades enter the picture. It is revealing to note that at no point did the crusaders attack the Muslim homeland, Arabia, but only those originally Christian territories that Muslims had conquered. In other words, if we want to use war terminology, the crusades to the East were in every way *defensive* wars, and certainly not aimed at Muslims as such. They were a direct response to Muslim acts—in an attempt to turn back or defend land against Muslim conquests. Some may call these Muslim activities simply "acts," but calling them "acts of aggression" is likely closer to the mark. One might say that Muslims acted like children who start fights and then complain when they lose.

Muslim expansion went on even after the crusades. The Turks were stopped from further European expansion at the Battle of Lepanto in 1571. Jerusalem itself was controlled by the Ottomans for another four hundred years, from 1516 until 1917, when British General Edmund Allenby liberated the city on December 11, 1917 near the end of World War I. Often called the Last Crusade, his expedition coincided with the Balfour Declaration on a homeland for Israel. The polarity between Christianity and Islam has lasted to this very day.

So it should not come as a surprise that the crusades have left a larger mark on Christians than on Muslims. Interestingly, the first Arabic history of the crusades was not written until 1899. The main reason for this lack of Muslim interest stemmed from the fact that the crusades were *not* successful in establishing the permanent liberation of the Holy Land. Not until widespread European colonialism followed the breakup of the Ottoman Turkish Empire in the early 20th century did the crusades come to be used as anti-imperialist propaganda. Mehmet Ali Agca, the man who attempted to assassinate Pope John Paul II, was infatuated with this false history as he stated, "I have decided to kill Pope John Paul II, supreme commander of the crusades."

Do We All Have the Same God?

Yet the question remains why we should wage war against another religion such as Islam. Are not Jews, Christians, and Muslims all descendants of Abraham? They all confess monotheism. So, don't we all pray to the same God? Isn't the only thing that matters in the dialog of religions a "common ground"—making the rest only a matter of mere trimmings?

Instead, we ought to consider the following question: is it really true that Christians and Muslims believe in the same God? In a very broad sense, this must be true, for there is, after all, only one God. Whether we pray to our Father in Heaven or to Allah, there is only one God who is paying attention to our prayers. But if that is so, then *anyone* who prays is praying to the same God to whom Catholics pray. So we end up with a rather trivial, empty statement. Of course, words like "God," "Dios," or "Dieu" are just different words in different languages for the same God. But it is doubtful whether words like "God," "Allah," and "Zeus" also refer to the same God. As Deuteronomy 6:4 puts it, "The Lord is our God, the Lord *alone*"—and no other gods.

From there on, the "same God" thesis begins to fall apart. Is it really true that our "common ground" is God—making the rest just a matter of irrelevant details? Or is God also in the details? In the confrontation between Christianity and Islam, we soon discover that the common ground approach ignores some essential differences between the two. Both religions presumably refer to the same God—in an abstract sense, that is—but the way they talk about this assumed common reference is very different. So they could very well be talking about two different "things." How can the Muslim God be the same as the God whom Christians adore? Yes, they both talk about "love of God and neighbor," but for Muslims this extends only to other Muslims. Human dignity in Islam comes from, and is conditional upon, belief in and practice of Islam. The Muslim God commands to kill or subjugate Jews and Christians, unless they accept the God of Islam. Allah curses anyone who says that God has a son. Allah allows and even promotes a morality of polygamy. The Muslim heaven is a man's haven where each man is rewarded with seventy-two beautiful, buxom virgins, plentiful food, slaves galore to attend to every whim and wish—a place so totally different from the Christian heaven where, in the words of Schoeman, "the bliss comes from the pure joy of being in God's presence; in Islam it comes from base sensual pleasures—food, drink, and sex" (p. 297).

Are these just details that do not really matter? The common ground approach begins to look more and more like thin ice. What we do have as a common ground is that we are all human beings, but the rest is not that obvious. The title of a recent book raises a very pertinent question: *Is the Father of Jesus the God of Muhammad?* Or are they perhaps essentially different? I am sure Muslims would ask similar questions—how could the God they adore be the same as the Christian God? Many Muslims even hold that belief in the Trinity disqualifies Christians from being monotheists. In other words, Muslims would never buy into the "common ground" myth—neither should Christians. Any kind of dialogue between religions must be honest about the differences that separate them— sparing us a false impression of common ground. Pope Benedict XVI's encyclical *Caritas in Veritate* ("Charity in Truth") clearly articulates that the aim of any dialogue between religions is ultimately *truth*. The aim for both sides should be to come to the truth, albeit through respect and love. We can and should agree to agreeably disagree. If Christians believe—as they do—that Jesus Christ is God's all-inclusive revelation, then there can be no correction or addition to it.

On the other hand, does respect for other religions not mean that we let go of any truth claims? Do we have to go along to get along? Those who think along such lines wrongly identify respect for people with respect for beliefs. Benedict XVI was right when he expressed a deep respect for Muslims, but that is not the same as having a deep respect for Islam. The latest interreligious prayer meeting in Assisi made unmistakably clear that gathering together to pray is not the same as praying together, for praying together implies that we are believing in the same God and are praying to the same God—which may not be the case. On the other hand, people from different religions, although they may have very different understandings of the divine, should come together to pray at the same time for the same intention—their longing for peace, for instance—but without praying together. Other religions may sometimes speak like Christians, but they often mean something very different.

When we speak of God, we may have very different understandings of what the term "God" stands for. In comparison, talking about "Venus" may refer for some to a planet, for some to a Greek goddess, for others to a horoscope. Does that mean we are all talking "the same thing"? Obviously, there is no common ground for these different interpretations. As to God, it certainly matters that we have different understandings of the divine. The way we understand God and know God determines and penetrates everything else we do in life. If we say we love God, we need to know who God is; for we cannot love what we do not know. In loving someone, we want to know that person—which is a cycle that never ends. We must know our faith with the same precision as specialists need to know their specific fields.

In fact, the concept of truth is at the core of all world religions, especially in Christianity. It is *true* that Jesus is the Son of God: "He has given all judgment to the Son, so that all will honor the Son even as they honor the Father. He who does not honor the Son does not honor the Father who sent Him" (John 5:22–23). If Jesus never existed, the Word did not become flesh. If Jesus did exist but was never crucified, we were not redeemed. And as the Apostle Paul wrote, "If there is no resurrection of the dead, then Christ has not been raised; if Christ has not been raised, then our preaching is in vain and your faith is in vain" (1 Cor. 15:13–14). Cardinal Avery Dulles referred to the idea that we could pursue unity by bypassing doctrine as a "blind alley." In his own words, "I call this solution false because the practice of the churches, as they engage in worship, moral teaching, and social advocacy, is intimately bound up with their doctrinal stands."

Once we start speaking about God, we begin to realize that our understandings of the divine can be quite divergent—and that is why religions can be so different. As a consequence, religions may have "something" in common, but not necessarily an equally valid path to the living God. Truth is truth, even if you do not accept it; and untruth is untruth, even if you claim it. In other words, religious conceptions may be right, or they may be wrong; but because God's transcendence is a true reality, we cannot just say about God whatever we choose.

The Battle for Jerusalem

Christian Claims on Jerusalem

Earlier we discussed that it is difficult to believe that the crusades could have attracted all the support they did without an extraordinary dedication to the ultimate objective, the liberation of the Holy City of Jerusalem for Christian pilgrims. To fortify this argument, it is helpful that we elucidate and explore the events which locate Jerusalem and the Holy Land as the heart and home of Israel and the Christian faith.

Jesus Christ was born in Bethlehem around the year 4 BC. His legal father Joseph was of the Israelite House of David (Luke 2:4) and his mother Mary was of Levitical descent through her cousin Elizabeth (Luke 1:5). Jesus Christ lived during the time of the Herodians, who served as vassal Kings for the Romans. The Holy Family fled to Egypt to avoid the Massacre of the Innocents (Matthew 2:13–15), but returned to Nazareth of Galilee after the death of Herod. Jesus visited the Jewish Temple of Jerusalem at age twelve with his parents during Passover (Luke 2:41–52). His adulthood lasted during the reign of the Roman Emperor Tiberius and the Procurator Pontius Pilate. St. John the Evangelist, with ties to the Jewish priesthood, records that Jesus went to Jerusalem during his ministry to attend three Passovers and also the Feast of the Dedication (John 10:23). Before his Passion and Crucifixion, Christ lamented over the fate of Jerusalem (Luke 19:41–44) and prophesied its destruction (Mark 13:2).

At the end of each of the Gospels, there are accounts of Jesus's Last Supper in an "Upper Room" in Jerusalem, his arrest in Gethsemane, his trial, his crucifixion at Golgotha, his burial nearby and his resurrection, ascension, and prophecy to return. Tradition holds that the place of the Last Supper is the Cenacle, on the second floor of a building on Mount Zion where David's Tomb is on the first floor. The place of Jesus's anguished prayer and betrayal, Gethsemane, is probably somewhere near the Church of All Nations on the Mount of Olives. Jesus's trial before Pontius Pilate may have taken place at the Antonia Fortress, to the north of the Temple area. The Acts of the Apostles and Pauline Epistles show St. James, the brother of Jesus, as leader of the early Jerusalem church. He and his successors were the focus for Jewish Christians until the destruction of the city by Emperor Hadrian in 135. In short, there is no doubt Jerusalem and the Holy Land serve as the home, not only of the Jewish faith, but also of the Christian faith.

It is no wonder, then, that Jerusalem has a special meaning for Christians. But during the first centuries, the time was not ready yet for intensive and extensive pilgrimages, until Constantine issued the Edict of Milan in 313 which ended Christian persecution. It was not until Constantine and his mother St. Helena restored Jerusalem in the 4th century that Christian pilgrimages to Jerusalem became safe for those who had the means to travel. After Hadrian's pagan temple was dismantled, St. Helena discovered the true Cross. She then ordered the construction of the Church of the Holy Sepulcher over the site of Christ's burial and Resurrection, which was completed in AD 335.

So there is no denying that Christians have a long lasting relationship with Jerusalem and the Holy Land, rooted in a centuries old tradition. Soon these places would become the favorite goal for many Catholics to make a pilgrimage to their favorite land and city—and when that was no longer possible, they tried to secure a way. Muslims speak out clearly when they perceive an attack on Islam. Why can't Christians speak out clearly when they perceive an attack on Christianity?

Today a fragile peace has settled over Jerusalem, with the presence of the world's three major religions (Judaism, Christianity, and Islam). Isn't it ironic that the city which is called "Jeru-Salem," or "City of Peace," has little peace to offer? Both the Jews and the Palestinians are locked in a bitter and endless struggle in their efforts to establish their respective homelands. History keeps repeating itself. There are Jewish claims on the Holy City, but also Christian claims and Islamic claims. How strong are these claims? If they are mutually exclusive, does anyone have to give in?

Muslim Claims on Jerusalem

Muhammad (AD 570–632), the founder of Islam, was born in Mecca as a member of the Quraysh tribe. He took flight to Medina in AD 622, known as the *Hejira*, but took to the sword and conquered Mecca in AD 630 and cleansed the *Kaaba* with the Black Stone of all idols and rededicated it to "the one true God." Mecca is the home of Islam to this very day.

The founding of Islam by Muhammad changed the complexion of the Middle East. The four Rightly Guided Caliphs were the immediate successors to Muhammad and rapidly expanded Islamic territory. The concept of holy war, or *jihad*, to further religious aims was eagerly embraced by the followers of Islam. The Muslims under the Caliph Umar captured Jerusalem in AD 638, and the Patriarchates of Jerusalem, Antioch, and Alexandria were placed under the control of the Caliphates.

So the question arises: What claim do Muslims have on Jerusalem? Islam's claims to the Holy City ultimately depend on the Temple Mount being the site from which Muhammad is said to have ascended to heaven in a dream, thus making Jerusalem the third holiest site of Islam. This ascent occurs in the seventeenth Sura in the Koran. It recounts that in a dream or vision Muhammad was taken by night "to the farthest mosque." The Arab world now considers "the farthest mosque" to be the Mosque of Omar on the Temple Mount.

It would seem that this is a legitimate, powerful claim which ends all discussion, except that reality is a little different. Schoeman makes the following comments on the Muslim claims regarding Jerusalem:

> [W]hen Muhammad died in AD 632, Jerusalem was still a Christian city and had no mosques at all. In fact, up until 638, when Jerusalem was captured by Khalif Omar, a Christian church known as Saint Mary of Justinian stood on the site. It was con-

verted into a mosque only around 711 by Abd El-Wahd, who ruled Jerusalem from 705–715. Thus not only is it certain that Muhammad was never physically present in Jerusalem, but the mosque on the Temple Mount to which he supposedly went was not built until three generations after his death. (pp. 283–84)

As a matter of fact, continues Schoeman,

> [t]he Arab world paid little attention to Jerusalem—or to the Temple Mount, for that matter—whenever they had uncontested possession to it. During the several centuries that the Temple Mount was held by the Muslim Turks, no repairs were done on the Dome of the Rock and the El-Aksa mosque. Photographs taken of them at the time show them in a state of disrepair, with missing roof tiles and high grass growing through the paving stones. . . . In contrast to its tenuous connection to Islam, Jerusalem is central to both Judaism and Christianity. It is mentioned numerous times in both the Old and the New Testament. . . . It is not mentioned a single time in the Koran.

In contrast, the Jerusalem Temple was built on the site where Melchizedek had offered bread and wine, where Abraham had offered his son, and where God had sworn his oath to save all nations. All Scriptural roads seem to lead to the city of King David, Mount Zion. Zion was also the place where Jesus instituted the Eucharist in the Upper Room, and where the Holy Spirit descended on Pentecost. The church on the site of these events survived the destruction of Jerusalem in AD 70.

In other words, both Judaism and Christianity have a strong connection with Jerusalem, whereas the Koran has much more ties with cities such as Medina and Mecca than with Jerusalem. Yet, Yassar Arafat would state in an interview on Palestinian television (June 28, 1998) that the issue of Jerusalem is a Palestinian and Islamic and Christian issue, not a Jewish issue at all, since the Jews consider Hebron to be holier than Jerusalem, or so he said. Unfortunately, what is essentially a religious issue has become a political issue again—in the same way as the religious crusades once became political crusades. If we do not learn from history, history tends to repeat itself.

Myth 3
The Catholic Inquisition

In the eyes of many, one of the greatest villains in Catholicism is the Inquisition. Interestingly enough, they never tell you which inquisition they are talking about. Usually, it is the *Spanish* Inquisition. They probably do not realize that the term "*the* Inquisition" represents a group of rather diverse institutions.

First there was the *Medieval* Inquisition, which was in effect from 1184 to the 1230s as a special court to curb the spread of heresy—in particular the heresy of the Albigensians (or Cathars) in southern France and the Waldensians in southern France and northern Italy. But at the end of the Middle Ages, the concept and scope of the Inquisition was significantly expanded to other European countries, resulting in the *Spanish* Inquisition (late 15th century)—which was under the control of the Spanish monarchy using local clergy—the *Portuguese* Inquisition (16th century), and the *Roman* Inquisition of the 16th century onwards, covering most of the Italian peninsula, Malta, and some isolated pockets of papal jurisdiction in other parts of Europe, including Avignon in France. Arguably the most famous case tried by the Roman Inquisition involved Galileo Galilei in 1633 (see Myth 4).

In more recent history, the Inquisition would survive as part of the Roman Curia. In 1908 the name of the Congregation became *The Sacred Congregation of the Holy Office*. After the Second Vatican Council, it was replaced (1965) by the *Congregation for the Doctrine of the Faith*, which governs vigilance in matters of faith.

All these different institutions had one thing in common: to combat heresy. But this is where the similarities end. When people speak of the atrocities of the Inquisition, they usually refer to the Spanish Inquisition. But even the Spanish Inquisition deserves neither the exaggerated praise nor the equally exaggerated vilification often bestowed on it, as we will see.

The Target of the Inquisition

Combatting Heresy

To begin with, we should emphasize that the target of the Inquisition was never any particular group outside Christianity, neither Jews nor Muslims, but Christianity itself, and more in particular its heretics. The primary task of the Inquisition was to keep the Church free of heresy. In other words, the Inquisition was supposed to investigate like the Federal Bureau of Investigation investigates in our own day. The Inquisition investigates as to whether there is danger within the Church—the danger being heresy.

Investigation means that the outcome can be positive or negative. The job of the Inquisition, then, is twofold: to detect heretics, but also to clear the good names of many people who were falsely accused of being heretics. Even some future saints were investigated. St. Joan of Arc was one of them. Later on, St. Ignatius of Loyola, the founder of the Jesuits, would twice become a focus of their investigations (the second time for his now-famous *Spiritual Exercises*), but in both cases he was cleared. And even the writings of Louis of Granada, the Provincial of the Dominicans in Portugal, caught the vigilant eye of the Inquisition for a short time.

The Medieval Inquisition began in 1184 when Pope Lucius III sent a list of heresies to Europe's bishops and commanded them to take an active role in determining whether those accused of heresy were, in fact, guilty or not. Rather than relying on secular courts, local lords, or just unruly mobs, bishops were to see to it that accused heretics in their dioceses were examined fairly by knowledgeable churchmen using Roman laws of evidence. In other words, they were to "inquire"—hence the term "inquisition."

In response to the failures of local inquisitions, the papal inquisition was staffed by trained inquisitors or judges recruited almost exclusively from the Dominican order. Because this religious order had been created to debate with heretics and preach the Catholic faith, the Dominicans especially became active in the Inquisition. Not only were these inquisitors endowed with the requisite knowledge, but they would also be most likely to do what seemed their duty for the good of the Church.

We know, for instance, that Dominicans were sent as inquisitors in 1232 to Germany along the Rhine, to the Diocese of Tarragona in Spain, and to Lombardy; in 1233 to France, to the territory of Auxerre, the ecclesiastical provinces of Bourges, Bordeaux, Narbonne, and Auch, and to Burgundy; in 1235 to the ecclesiastical province of Sens. Around 1255, we find Inquisition activities in full force in all the countries of Central and Western Europe—in the county of Toulouse, in Sicily, Aragon, Lombardy, France, Burgundy, Brabant, and Germany.

Another reason for the creation of the Medieval Inquisition was to bring order and legality to the process of dealing with heresy, since there had been tendencies in the mobs of townspeople to burn alleged heretics without the process of a trial. The pope did not establish the Inquisition as a distinct and separate tribunal, though; what he did do was to appoint special but permanent judges, who executed their doctrinal functions in his name. Where they sat, there was the Inquisition.

A third reason for the pope's initiative was related to the issue of separation between Church and State. Pope Gregory IX was anxious to block the aspirations of Frederick II in strictly ecclesiastical matters of doctrine. We need only recall the hereditary passion of the Hohenstaufen dynasty for supreme control over Church and State, claiming God-given authority over both. For this purpose it would seem necessary for the Pope to establish a distinct and specifically *ecclesiastical* court. For centuries, the European states had been more eager to manage the affairs of the Church than the Church had been to intrude in civil matters. Popes, bishops, and abbots often were treated as vassals of kings and emperors, serving as their ministers and carrying out their commands. Pope Gregory IX was going to change this with his Inquisition.

We need to emphasize that there was no central office in the Medieval Inquisition, no overarching authority, not even papal oversight. A vast, papal-controlled, grand, and singular Inquisition never really existed in Europe—it is a fabrication. Local bishops or members of the mendicant orders established ecclesial courts for the investigation of heresy. They used procedures rather common to secular legal procedures. However, regional control of the inquisition process would become more prevalent. What had begun in the 13th century as a papal-designated juridical system to remove "heresy-hunting" from control of the mob or secular authorities evolved rather quickly as a device of the local Church and secular authorities to address local, and, later, national or dynastic goals. As a result, there were many inquisitions, rather than "the Inquisition," singular.

One of these was the Spanish Inquisition—probably the worst villain in the imaginations of anti-Catholics. The Spanish Inquisition properly begins with the reign of King Ferdinand II of Aragon and Queen Isabella I of Castile. The Catholic faith was then endangered by what some considered pseudo-converts from Judaism (*marranos*) and Islam (*moriscos*). On November 1, 1478, Sixtus IV empowered the Catholic sovereigns to set up their own Inquisition. The judges were to be at least forty years old, of impeccable reputation, distinguished for virtue and wisdom, masters of theology, or doctors or licentiates of canon law, and needed to be obedient to the usual ecclesiastical rules and regulations. On September 17, 1480, Their Catholic Majesties appointed, at first for Seville, the two Dominicans Miguel de Morillo and Juan de San Martin as inquisitors, with two assistants of the secular clergy.

However, someone else, Fray Tomás Torquemada, would become the true organizer—and for many the true villain—of the Spanish Inquisition. In 1483, at the solicitation of Their Spanish Majesties, Pope Sixtus IV bestowed on Torquemada the office of Grand Inquisitor, the institution of which indicates a decided new step in the development of the Spanish Inquisition. It was Torquemada's job to establish rules of evidence and procedure for the Inquisition as well as to set up branches in major cities. Pope Sixtus confirmed the appointment, hoping that it would bring some order to the situation. Pope Innocent VIII approved the act of his predecessor in 1487, and Torquemada was given dignity of Grand Inquisitor for the kingdoms of Castile, Leon, Aragon, Valencia, etc. The institution speedily ramified from Seville to Cordova, Jaén, Villareal, and Toledo.

The procedure of the Spanish Inquisition was substantially the same as for most other inquisitions. A "term of grace" of thirty to forty days was invariably granted, and was often prolonged. Imprisonment resulted only when unanimity had been arrived at or the offence had been proved. Examination of the accused could take place only in the presence of two impartial priests, whose obligation it was to restrain any arbitrary act in their presence; the protocol had to be read out twice to the accused. The defense lay always in the hands of a lawyer. The witnesses, although unknown to the accused, were sworn, and very severe punishment, even death, awaited false witnesses.

A Different Assessment

Many unfavorable assessments regarding the Inquisition have been made, especially with regard to the Spanish Inquisition. These assessments have a long history. But are they impartial, or are they perhaps skewed by grave prejudices?

It is fair to say that groups targeted by inquisitors tried hard to spread a negative image of the Inquisition as an institution. It is also fair to say that a new wave of heretics, the Protestants, had a potent new weapon against their inquisitors: the printing press. This weapon would soon be used especially in the "war" between Catholic Spain—with its King Philip II, who saw himself and his countrymen as faithful defenders of the Catholic Church—and the less wealthy and less powerful Protestant areas of Europe. The Protestant revolt in Germany and England had rapidly eaten its way into Holland, Belgium, France, Switzerland, and Czechoslovakia. Although the Spanish defeated Protestants on the battlefield, they would lose the propaganda war. These were the years when the famous "Black Legend" of Spain was forged. Innumerable books and pamphlets poured from northern presses accusing the Spanish Empire, including its Inquisition, of horrible atrocities. They created an image of the Spanish Inquisition as the epitome of Catholic terror and barbarity. From the 16th through the early 20th century, the legend of the inquisition grew larger than its history.

This legend still persists today in the imagination of many, despite its debunking by historians. What was the breeding ground for this legend? In Germany in 1567, two Spanish Protestants under the pseudonym Reginaldus Gonzalvus Montanus published *Sanctae Inquisitionis Hispanicae Artes*. Though a basic propaganda tract, it would be reprinted throughout Europe and be considered the definitive source on the Inquisition for over 200 years. Most Inquisition "histories" written thereafter, virtually until the late 19th century, would rely on Montanus's work, which became a primary source, though written by anything but an unbiased eye.

The true explosion in Inquisition rhetoric was in the periods just prior to and during the revolt of the Netherlands against Spanish control. That revolt involved a fragile alliance of Catholic and Calvinist leaders against Catholic Spain. Though the Dutch themselves were trying heretics with their own state-run inquisition, it was argued that King Philip II of Spain (who succeeded Charles V) was to introduce specifically a Spanish Inquisition in the Netherlands, not only crushing Protestants but denying Catholics their own freedoms as well—hence the alliance.

It is time to correct this propaganda campaign with a different assessment. There is no denying that by the 14th century the Inquisition represented the best legal practices available. Inquisition officials were university-trained specialists in law and theology. Not only would a purely spiritual or papal religious tribunal protect the accused from mob trials and secular courts, but it would also secure ecclesiastical liberty, since authority for this court could be entrusted to men of expert knowledge and blameless reputation, and above all to independent men in whose hands the Church could trust the decision as to the orthodoxy or heterodoxy of a given teaching.

It must also be carefully noted that the characteristic feature of the Inquisition was not its peculiar procedure, nor the secret examination of witnesses and consequent official indictment—these features were common to all European courts from the time of Pope Innocent III. Nor was it the torture, which was not prescribed or even allowed for decades after the beginning of the Inquisition, nor, lastly, the various sanctions, imprisonment, confiscation, stake burning, etc.—all of which were customary punishments long before the Inquisition. The inquisitor, strictly speaking, was a special but permanent judge acting in the name of the pope and clothed by him with the right and the duty to deal legally with offences against the Faith; he was expected, however, to adhere to the established rules of canonical procedure and pronounce the customary penalties.

Because of all of this, it must be stated that the Inquisition was not born out of desire to crush diversity or oppress people, but was rather a dual attempt: to identify real heresies and to stop unjust executions. Heresy was considered a crime against the State; Roman law in the Code of Justinian made it a capital offense. Civil rulers, whose authority was believed to come from God, had no patience for heretics. Neither did common people, who saw them as dangerous outsiders who would bring down divine wrath. When someone was accused of heresy in the early Middle Ages, they were brought to the local lord for judgment, just as if they had committed theft or vandalism. Yet in contrast to those crimes, it was not so easy to discern whether the accused was really a heretic.

To make such a discernment, one needed some basic theological training—something most medieval lords very much lacked, not to mention the mobs. The result is that uncounted thousands across Europe used to be executed by secular authorities without fair trials or a competent assessment of the validity of the charge. The Inquisition, on the other hand, provided a means for heretics to escape death and return to the community. While medieval secular leaders were trying to safeguard their kingdoms, the Church was trying to save souls. Saving souls meant that convicted heretics were given a chance to repent, to change their beliefs, and to get back in the fold of their Church. Only if that did not work, they were handed over to civil authorities. By doing so, the inquisitors were able to keep their hands clean.

As a consequence, imprisonment was not always punishment in the proper sense: it was rather looked on as an opportunity for repentance, a preventive against backsliding or infecting others. I am not whitewashing the history of the Inquisition. The Inquisition did exist and it remains an unsettling part of Catholic history. However, the caricature of the Inquisition that most of us are familiar with and that is often utilized in anti-Catholic polemics has little to do with the full reality of the Inquisition. But there is more to it.

Why Did the Inquisition Target the Jews?

Pogroms and Anti-Semitism

Since the Spanish Inquisition is often a particular object of anti-Catholic propaganda, we will focus on that particular kind of inquisition. It grew out of the specific local situation in Spain. It had very little involvement with trials and punishments of Protestants—in spite of centuries of propaganda to the contrary—but was, in the general perception, mainly connected with pogroms and anti-Semitism. We need to carefully examine that presumed connection.

Portugal and Spain in the late Middle Ages consisted largely of multicultural territories of Muslim and Jewish influence retaken (reconquista) from the control of Islamic forces. Medieval Spain had the single largest Jewish community in the world, numbering some 100,000 souls in the 13th century. For centuries, Jews and Christians had lived and worked in a rather peaceful, though generally segregated, co-existence. In the 14th century, however, anti-Jewish attitudes were on the rise throughout Europe. In 1290, England expelled its Jews, and France followed in 1306. Spain also began to experience an increasing anti-Jewish sentiment which exploded in the summer of 1391 with angry anti-Jewish riots. In the pogroms of June 1391 in Seville, hundreds of Jews were killed, and the synagogue was completely destroyed. The number of people killed was also high in other cities, such as Córdoba, Valencia, and Barcelona.

Since these riots were more religious than racial, they led to major forced conversions of Jews to Christianity. These Jewish converts would be called *conversos*, or more scornfully *marranos*, in order to distinguish them from traditional Christian families. However, the Christian authorities could not assume that all their new subjects would suddenly become and remain orthodox Catholics. So the Inquisition in Iberia, in the lands of the Reconquista counties, and kingdoms such as Leon, Castile, and Aragon, had a special socio-political basis as well as more fundamental religious motives.

Keep in mind, though, that forced baptism has always been contrary to the law of the Catholic Church, and theoretically anybody who had been forcibly baptized had the legal right to return to Judaism. Although there were legal definitions of the time that the-

75

oretically acknowledged that a forced baptism was not a valid sacrament, such definitions were sometimes very narrowly interpreted and confined to cases where baptism was administered literally by physical force. Hence, even a person who had consented to baptism under mere threat of death or serious injury was still regarded as a voluntary convert and accordingly forbidden to revert to Judaism. No wonder, after the public violence, many of the converted felt it safer to remain in their new religion.

Over the years, the "Old Christians" began to see the new converts as opportunists who secretly maintained the faith of their forefathers. It was this religious prejudice against the *conversos* that would entice King Ferdinand II of Aragon and Queen Isabella I of Castile to establish the Spanish Inquisition in 1478. In contrast to the previous inquisitions, it operated completely under *royal* authority, though staffed by clergy and order members, but independently of the Holy See. It operated in Spain and in all Spanish colonies and territories, which included the Canary Islands, the Spanish Netherlands, the Kingdom of Naples, and all Spanish possessions in North, Central, and South America.

Especially when Torquemada came to be the Grand Inquisitor, the Spanish Inquisition became infected with inhuman cruelty. Because the Spanish Inquisition had no jurisdiction over the Jews in Spain, Torquemada urged the sovereigns to compel all the Jews either to become Christians or to leave Spain. To frustrate his designs, the Jews agreed to pay the Spanish government 30,000 ducats if left unmolested. But Torquemada expressed his objection to such a deal. Chiefly through his intervention, the Jews were officially expelled from Spain in 1492.

While many Jews fled, a large number converted, thus aggravating the popular picture of secret Judaizers within the Christian community of Spain. Although the Spanish Inquisition had been universally established in Spain a few years prior to the expulsion of the Jews, its records indicate that virtually the only "heresy" prosecuted at that time was the alleged secret practice of the Jewish faith by pseudo-converts. Some claim that, during Torquemada's office (1483–1498), 8,800 suffered death by fire and 9,654 were punished in other ways. However, these figures are highly exaggerated; most scholars hold with the Protestant historian Peschel that approximately 2,000 "heretics" were turned over to the secular authorities for execution from 1481 until 1504 (the year that Isabella died)—which is certainly not a nice record, but at least more accurate.

Some link Columbus's activities to these events. They have postulated that Columbus was of Iberian Jewish origins (not Italian). As a matter of fact, Columbus always wrote in Spanish, and occasionally included Hebrew in his writing, and referenced the Jewish High Holidays in his journal during the first voyage. There are clear indications that Columbus had apocalyptic beliefs. He was trying to find gold to take Jerusalem back from the Muslims before the end of the world. Simon Wiesenthal, the famous Nazi hunter, goes one step further and postulates that Columbus was in fact a Sephardic Jew, careful to conceal his Judaism, yet also eager to locate a place of refuge for his persecuted fellow countrymen. Wiesenthal even argues that Columbus's concept of sailing west to reach the Indies was less the result of geographical theories than of his faith in certain Biblical texts—specifically the Book of Isaiah.

The Other Side of the Story

Because of its strong focus on people of Jewish descent, the Spanish Inquisition has often been accused of anti-Semitism. To answer the question as to whether anti-Semitism is the ultimate motive behind the work of the Spanish Inquisition, we need to make some distinctions.

In the past, unfortunately, there have been many persecutions of the Jews in Christian countries. Schoeman distinguishes three categories of persecutions of the Jews (pp. 179–81). Some were mob actions, inflamed expressions of blood lust and fury, like we saw them sometimes during the crusades but also during the time of the inquisitions. Often they were incited by pseudo-Catholic exhortations to avenge the death of Christ. Although not caused by the Inquisition, mob actions did occur in Spain. During the summer of 1391, for instance, urban mobs in Barcelona and other towns poured into Jewish quarters, rounded up Jews, and gave them a choice of baptism or death. Most took baptism. The king of Aragon, who had done his best to stop the attacks, later reminded his subjects of well-established Church doctrine on the matter of forced baptisms—they are invalid. He decreed that any Jews who accepted baptism to avoid death could return to their religion. In addition, the papacy would continue to complain about the treatment of the *conversos*, but soon the strong alliance between the Spanish Inquisition and the State would become a disturbing factor and sever ties with Rome

The second category of Catholic persecutions of the Jews is represented by laws and actions that were aimed at getting Jews to convert to Christianity. It was believed at the time that there was no possibility of heaven for the unbaptized, so it was considered an act of charity to the Jews to do everything possible to bring them to convert to Christianity and thus save them from damnation. Again, the Inquisition itself did not have this aim; it had no jurisdiction over Jews, so it could certainly not force them to convert to Christianity. Interestingly enough, Spanish rabbis after 1391 had considered *conversos* to still be Jews, since they had been forced into baptism. Yet by 1414, most rabbis repeatedly stressed that *conversos* were indeed true Christians, since they had voluntarily left Judaism.

The third category consists of campaigns to produce a Christian society and a Christian state. The expulsion of the Jews from Spain in 1492 falls into this category. Baptized—that is, converted—Jews were always welcome and exempt from persecution. As Schoeman puts it,

> In order to avoid the forced expulsion from Spain, a large number of Jewish families had pretended to convert to Catholicism, while continuing to practice the Jewish religion in secret. It was these "crypto"-Jews who were targets of the Inquisition, not as Jews—for the Inquisition always acknowledged that it had no authority at all over non-Christians—but as heretical Christians. As a fight against heresy and sacrilege within the Catholic Church, the Inquisition pursued only Christians. The Marranos, by participating in the sacraments and pretending to be Christian, fell into the purview of the Inquisition. They were unfortunately also heretics because of their Jewish beliefs and committed sacrilege whenever they participated in the sacraments. This brought the wrath of the inquisition down upon them. Yet it was not based on their being Jewish, but on their being false Catholics. (p. 180)

Did the Spanish Inquisition always play by the rules? Certainly not. Therefore, Torquemada's successor, the cardinal archbishop of Toledo, Francisco Jimenez de Cisneros, worked hard to reform the Inquisition, removing corrupt authorities and reforming procedures. Once these reforms had been implemented, the Spanish Inquisition had very few critics. Staffed by well-educated legal professionals, it was one of the most efficient and compassionate judicial bodies in Europe. As historian Thomas Madden has written: "the Spanish Inquisition was widely hailed as the best run, most humane court in Europe."

Yet, criticism of the Inquisition remains. The argument is that the Catholic Church cannot possibly be a "good" or "true" Church, let alone a "holy" Church," because it has done some terrible things. However, a condemnation like this arises from a fundamental misunderstanding of the nature of Christ's Church: the Church is not identical to the people in the Church. The Catholic Church is pure and holy in its teachings and its sacraments; but nobody ever claimed that all of its members or even all of its clergy are perfect and sinless—such a claim would be completely off the mark. The evil actions of the Inquisition were the actions of individual Church members, not of the Church herself.

Where Did the Inquisition Go Astray?

Jews, Protestants, and Witches

In popular perception, the victims of the Catholic Inquisition were Jews, Protestants, and witches. How accurate is that perception?

Were Jews the target of the Inquisition? We discussed already that even the Spanish Inquisition had no authority over Jews, but it did investigate so-called conversos who had "joined" the Catholic Church for "political" reasons while remaining Jewish in their convictions and practices. They were not targeted for being Jews, but for possibly being quasi-Christians.

Were Protestants targeted by the Inquisition? Yes, they were, especially by the German Inquisition. However, the Protestants in Germany had their own "inquisitions" as well. One of their regular inquisitions was set up in Saxony, for instance, with Melanchthon on the bench; under it many persons were punished, some with death, some with life imprisonment, and some with exile. There is strong evidence that the Protestant "witch" burnings in Germany alone killed more people than the various actions of the Inquisition in Catholic Europe all combined. When Protestants read blood-curdling stories of the Inquisition and of atrocities committed by the Catholic Inquisition, they often forget about the Protestant atrocities in the centuries succeeding the Reformation.

As a side note, it must be stressed that the Spanish Inquisition never really investigated Protestants. The image of a Spanish Inquisition burning hundreds of thousands of Protestant heretics has no basis in historical fact but is a creation of the presses running in Northern Europe. There were so few Protestants in Spain at the time that there could be no such prosecution, no matter how strong the Inquisition was and no matter how much anti-Catholic propagandists tried to create such an image in the 16th century and thereafter.

Next we must ask, were witches investigated by the Inquisition? The answer is a cautious "yes." When the first accusations of witchcraft surfaced in northern Spain, the Inquisition sent its people to investigate. However, these trained legal scholars did *not* find any believable evidence for witches' Sabbaths, black magic, or baby roasting.

It must be admitted, though, that during what is known as the Little Ice Age, Pope Innocent VIII, in his 1484 papal bull *Summis Desiderantes Affectibus* had instigated severe measures against magicians and witches in Germany. In the popular perception, the grip of freezing weather, failing crops, rising crime, and mass starvation was blamed not on the Little Ice Age but on witches. So the Pope asked the inquisitors Heinrich Kramer and Jacobus Sprenger to systemize the persecution of witches. These two would later write the *Malleus Maleficarum* in 1486, which stated that witchcraft was to blame for bad weather. In 1490, however, the Vatican decided that the book was false, and in 1538 the Spanish Inquisition explicitly cautioned against using it.

Yet, for a while, the inquisition did focus on the so-called "popular religion" of superstitious practices, including witchcraft, which had survived in the 15th and 16th centuries. Unlike the Protestant reformers, however, the inquisitions in both Italy and Spain eventually began to see these difficulties as the result of poor catechesis, rather than active heresy, and took less interest in its prosecution. More and more, the inquisitions turned rather skeptical toward accusations of witchcraft and sorcery, and established rigorous rules of prosecution and evidence. In most Catholic countries in the 17th century and beyond, the inquisitions had less and less to do with prosecution of superstition, whereas Protestant nations kept continuing their witch trials. The Salem Witch Trials in America are ultimately another consequence of all of this. In general one could say that countries which had dissolved their ties with the Roman Catholic Church had witch-trials conducted by secular courts under the control of the Protestant Reformers.

In spite of all of the above, there were abuses in the way inquisitions were handled. The abuses were more frequent when the State co-opted its powers to further its own interests, nowhere more so than in Spain, where inquisitors sought out signs of disloyalty to the Crown. Before long, complaints of grievous abuses reached Rome, and were only too well founded. In a 1482 Brief of Sixtus IV, the Inquisition was blamed for having unjustly imprisoned many people, subjected them to cruel tortures, declared them false believers, and sequestrated the property of the executed. Inquisitors were at first admonished to act only in conjunction with the bishops, and finally were threatened with deposition, and would indeed have been deposed had not Their Majesties in Spain interceded for them.

As the Spanish Inquisition expanded into Aragon, the hysteria levels reached new heights. Pope Sixtus IV attempted again to put a stop to it. On April 18, 1482, he wrote to the bishops of Spain:

> In Aragon, Valencia, Mallorca, and Catalonia the Inquisition has for some time been moved not by zeal for the faith and the salvation of souls but by lust for wealth. Many true and faithful Christians, on the testimony of enemies, rivals, slaves, and other lower and even less proper persons, have without any legitimate proof been thrust into secular prisons, tortured and condemned as relapsed heretics, deprived of their goods and property and handed over to the secular arm to be executed, to the peril of souls, setting a pernicious example, and causing disgust to many.

King Ferdinand was outraged when he heard of the letter. He wrote to Pope Sixtus, openly suggesting that the Pope had been bribed with *conversos'* gold:

> Things have been told me, Holy Father, which, if true, would seem to merit the greatest astonishment. . . . To these rumors, however, we have given no credence because they seem to be things which would in no way have been conceded by Your Holiness who has a duty to the Inquisition. But if by chance concessions have been made through the persistent and cunning persuasion of the conversos, I intend never to let them take effect. Take care therefore not to let the matter go further, and to revoke any concessions and entrust us with the care of this question.

That was the end of the papacy's role in the Spanish Inquisition. From then on, it would be an arm of the Spanish monarchy alone, separate from ecclesiastical authority. It is odd, then, that the Spanish Inquisition is so often today described as one of the Catholic Church's greatest sins. In fact, the Papacy and the Catholic Church as an institution had not much to do with its operations.

Torture and Execution

How did the Inquisition come to its verdicts? The Medieval Inquisition courts often functioned the way circuit courts have operated in the more recent past. Trials were held only for those who refused to confess under the period of grace. For those who returned to the Church, forgiveness was granted and some form of penance imposed. Those that did not reject their heresies were excommunicated and turned over to the secular authorities. For the most part, these courts functioned similarly to their secular counterparts at that time, although their sentences and penances were generally far less harsh.

The kinds and degrees of punishments inflicted by the Spanish Inquisition were also similar to those of the Medieval Inquisition—again, often lighter than those meted out by secular courts. It is equally true that many people preferred to have their cases tried by ecclesiastical courts because the secular courts had even fewer safeguards. In fact, historians have found records of people intentionally blaspheming in secular courts so they could have their case transferred to an ecclesiastical court, where they would get a better hearing.

Torture was rather common throughout Europe in regular judicial actions, so the Inquisition was no exception. It had become an element in the testimony of otherwise dubious witnesses, and a procedure could be triggered by enough partial proofs to indicate that a full proof—a confession—was likely, and no other full proofs were available. The procedure of torture itself was guarded by a number of protocols and protections for the defendant, and the jurists rigorously defined its place in due process. A confession made after or under torture had to be freely repeated the next day without torture, or it would have been considered invalid. Technically, therefore, torture was strictly a means of obtaining the only full proof available. It was Pope Innocent IV's papal bull *Ad Extirpanda* of 1252 that explicitly defined the appropriate circumstances for the use of torture by the Inquisition for eliciting confessions from heretics. Pope Clement V additionally ordained that inquisitors should not apply torture without the consent of the diocesan bishop.

In other words, torture was used to elicit confessions when there was insufficient proof, but under rules much stricter than the norm in secular courts of the time. Torture could only be used in cases of heresy and it was not used to punish, as was common in the secular courts. From the perspective of secular authorities, heretics were traitors to God and king, and therefore deserved death. From the perspective of the Church, on the other hand, heretics were lost sheep that had strayed from the flock. As shepherds, the Pope and Bishops had a duty to bring those sheep back into the fold, just as the Good Shepherd had commanded them. So, while medieval secular leaders were trying to safeguard their kingdoms, the Church was trying to save souls. Therefore, the inquisition provided a means for heretics to escape death and return to the community.

Like all courts in Europe, the Spanish Inquisition used torture as well, but it did so much less often than its counterparts. Modern researchers have discovered that the Spanish Inquisition applied torture in only two percent of its cases. Each instance of torture was limited to a maximum of fifteen minutes. In only one percent of the cases was torture applied twice, and never for a third time. True, torture was applied too frequently and too cruelly, but certainly not more cruelly than under Charles V's system of judicial torture in Germany. The commonly encountered lists of gruesome instruments of torture are the invention of post-Reformation propaganda rather than the reality of the Catholic inquisitions.

Did the Inquisition ever *execute* those who were found guilty of heresy? No, it did not. Its harshest penalties were imprisonment in its various degrees and exclusion from the communion of the Church. But that is where its punishments ended. The final step could be—but only for unrepentant, obstinate, or relapsed heretics—to turn over such cases to the civil, secular authorities who had the power to execute people, usually by burning them at the stake. The regular expression for such heretics was, "since the Church can no farther punish their misdeeds, she leaves them to the civil authority."

So, despite popular myth, the Church did *not* burn heretics. It was the secular authorities that held heresy to be a capital offense. The simple fact is that the Inquisition saved uncounted thousands of innocent (and even not-so-innocent) people who would otherwise have been roasted by secular lords or mob rule. Pope Gregory IX, known for instituting the Papal Inquisition in response to the failures of the episcopal inquisitions, continued to insist on the exclusive right of the Church to decide in authentic manner in matters of heresy, but at the same time, stressed it was not her office to pronounce sentence of death. The Church, from then on, expelled from her bosom the impenitent heretics, whereupon the State took over the duty of their temporal punishment.

Did execution at the stake happen often? Only relatively few people suffered at the stake during the Medieval Inquisition. Between 1308 and 1323, the Inquisitor Bernard Guy, who cannot be accused of inactivity, only handed over to the secular arm 42 persons, out of 930 who were convicted of heresy. But even after the bitter persecution of the *conversos* during the first 20 years of the Spanish Inquisition, executions were rare; in the 17th and 18th centuries fewer than three people a year were executed throughout Spain. No major court in Europe executed fewer people than the Spanish Inquisition. Nevertheless, many Catholic churchmen pointed out that it was contrary to all accepted practices for heretics to be burned without instruction in the Faith. If the *conversos*, for instance, were guilty at all, it must have been, so they reasoned, merely because of ignorance, not willful heresy.

There was opposition, it should be noted, to the Spanish Inquisition from inside the Church. Numerous clergy at the highest levels complained to King Ferdinand about abuses. Opposition to the Spanish Inquisition also continued in Rome. Pope Sixtus's successor, Innocent VIII, wrote twice to King Ferdinand asking for greater compassion, mercy, and leniency for the *conversos*. There was clearly some controversy within the Church about the inquisitions. They may have had a legitimate role within the Church, but nevertheless they were open to abuses, in spite of many built-in safeguards. And let us not forget about this rule: What the Church considers right may not be followed by all her members, so what an individual Church member, even an inquisitor, does may not be right according to the Church.

The Problem of Heresy

The Danger of Heresy

To give the Inquisition a fair assessment, we need to find out why heresy is such a threat to the Catholic Church and should be properly investigated.

Especially nowadays, many tend to see heresy in terms of a violation of "freedom of expression." In this assessment, there are no heretical views—they are merely harmless, perhaps dissident, alternative views. In science, no one would defend such a position: saying that disinfection before surgery makes no sense is not just an alternative view but is definitely "anathema" in science. Something similar holds for heresy in religion—it is anathema. Sometimes a heresy is an untruth, but often it is a faulty, partial truth—not a total lie but a firmly held half-truth that needs to be contested.

This is not to say that there was nothing evil in the Inquisition. But it certainly was not pure evil, as some claim, because its purpose was to rout out heresy. The Bible is very explicit about heresy—for instance, in Deuteronomy 17:2–5:

If there is found among you, within any of your towns which the Lord your God gives you, a man or woman who does what is evil in the sight of the Lord your God, in transgressing his covenant, and has gone and served other gods and worshiped them, or the sun or the moon or any of the host of heaven, which I have forbidden, and it is told you and you hear of it; then you shall inquire diligently [note the phrase "inquire diligently"], and if it is true and certain that such an abominable thing has been done in Israel, then you shall bring forth to your gates that man or woman who has done this evil thing, and you shall stone that man or woman to death with stones.

In the New Testament, the Apostles were deeply imbued with the conviction that they must transmit the deposit of the Faith to posterity undefiled, and that any teaching at variance with their own would be a culpable offense that would warrant exclusion from the communion of the Church (1 Timothy 1:20; Titus 3:10). From very early on, the New Testament tells us how the Christian community was forced to confront those people who persisted in teachings contrary to the Apostolic Faith. St. Paul is very adamant that heresies do and will arise within the church. In Acts 20: 29–30, his farewell to the Ephesian elders, he says,

I know that after my departure fierce wolves will come in among you, not sparing the flock; and from among your own selves will arise men speaking perverse things, to draw away the disciples after them.

In the Letter of St. John (1 John 2:19), it is stated that heresy always starts within the Christian family:

They went out from us, but they were not of us; for if they had been of us, they would have continued with us; but they went out, that it might be plain that they are not of us.

The implication is clear that heresy begins within the circle of Christian truth and doctrine. That is where heresies have their root. That is also what the word "antichrist" suggests. We often take the term to mean someone who is against Christ, much like the attitude we see in Communism, where there is a blatant denial of God and Christ. But that is not the thought here. It is true that the eventual outcome of any antichrist is that he is against Christ, but the word really means "instead of Christ." It is someone who comes in Christ's name, someone who declares that he or she is a Christian and is declaring the truth of Christianity. Yet, once we analyze his or her teaching, it turns out to be contrary to what God, in Christ, has said. This person is antichrist.

In the early centuries of Christendom various kinds of heresies rapidly emerged. One of them was Gnosticism, which claimed to have access to a secret source of religious knowledge that can bring salvation all by itself. Early Church Fathers such as St. Justin Martyr, Origen, St. Hippolytus, and St. Irenaeus identified the errors of Gnosticism and condemned Gnostic teachings as heretical. Gnosticism is certainly not a heresy from ages past; it is very alive in New Age-like movements. Pope Francis gives us a timeless description of Gnosticism in his 2013 Apostolic Exhortation *Evangelii Gaudium* (#94) as "a purely subjective faith whose only interest is a certain experience or a set of ideas and bits of information which are meant to console and enlighten, but which ultimately keep one imprisoned in his or her own thoughts and feelings."

Another heresy that appeared in early Christian times was Arianism, which regards Jesus not as a Son of God but as a created being. Arianism was condemned as a heresy by the Council of Nicaea in 325 and by the Council of Constantinople of 381. And then there was Manichaeism, which says "matter" is evil, thus denying the omnipotence of God and postulating two opposite powers, Good and Evil, which are in permanent conflict with each other. It spread with extraordinary rapidity in both East and West and maintained a sporadic and intermittent existence in Africa, Spain, France, Northern Italy, and the Balkans for a thousand years. St. Augustine was under its influence for almost ten years before he converted to Christianity.

Expelled from Rome and Milan, Manichaeism would stay dormant for a long time and finally came back in a new disguise as Catharism. Catharism was a blend of Gnosticism and of Manichaeism. Not only were the beliefs of Catharism heretical, they also entailed serious social consequences, detrimental to civilization. Marriage was scorned because it legitimized sexual relations, which Catharists identified as original sin. But fornication was permitted because it was temporary, secret, and was not generally approved of, whereas marriage was permanent, open, and publicly sanctioned. The ramifications of such theories are not hard to imagine. In addition, ritualistic suicide was encouraged (those who would not take their own lives were frequently "helped" along), and Catharists refused to take oaths, which, in a feudal society, meant they opposed all governmental authority.

Thus, Catharism was a religious, moral, and political danger at the same time. During the beginning of the thirteenth century, Christian Europe became so endangered by this heresy, and penal legislation concerning Catharism had gone so far, that the Inquisition seemed to be a political necessity. Had Catharism become dominant, or even had it been allowed to exist on equal terms with Catholicism, its influence could not have failed to become disastrous. It has been said that more perished through the suicide code of Catharism than through the Inquisition. It was, therefore, natural enough for the custodians of the Christian heritage and the existing social order in Europe to adopt repressive measures against such revolutionary teachings—which was the beginning of the Inquisition.

In matters of religion, the modern conception is that religion is a highly private issue. We tend to believe in whatever our conscience tells us to believe. Truth has become a private, relative issue. This new view is called relativism: the philosophical position that all truth is relative to the individual. It is the absolute doctrine that there are no absolute truths. Truth is what my "personal conscience" tells me it is. We find a comparable view among the Reformers, telling us that we can go by our own intuitions of Faith and our own interpretations of Scripture. *My* truth is supposed to be *the* truth.

However, conscience is not a private "compass" that determines its own North Pole. A real compass functions as a pointer to the magnetic north because the magnetized needle aligns itself with the lines of the Earth's magnetic field. It should not be used in proximity to ferrous metal objects or electromagnetic fields as that can affect their accuracy. At sea, for instance, a ship's compass must be corrected for errors, called deviation, caused by iron and steel in its structure and equipment. In a similar way, our "compass" has to be calibrated to the one and only real "North Pole," so it is in line with the directions of the Church.

We cannot give in to the absolute dictatorship of relativism, for relativists defy themselves when they make the absolute statement that everything is relative. Ironically, even relativists hold on to at least one absolute that says "Never disobey your own conscience." So we should ask relativists where the absolute authority of their private conscience comes from. If our conscience were merely a private issue that we form at our own discretion, it could never claim any absolute authority, for disagreements between two people could never be settled on the level of each person's private, personal, and infallible conscience. If such were the case, there would be a tie, for instance, between the conscience of a pro-choice pregnant mother and the conscience of her pro-life obstetrician. Each "private" conscience must ultimately be under a higher authority—the Church's, but ultimately God's. Truth is truth, even if you do not accept it; and untruth is untruth, even if you claim it.

The Catholic Church tells us very clearly that our conscience can be understood only in relation to the individual's duty to obey the Creator and his divine law—instead of leading our own lives as we please. Man's conscience "is man's most secret core and his sanctuary. There he is alone with God whose voice echoes in his depths" (CCC 1776). Man's conscience participates in God's knowing. In other words, the individual's conscience does not speak on its own but merely reflects the law spoken by God. That is the reason why we cannot take our conscience as an entirely private issue that we can form at our own discretion. A "dialogue" with oneself would only amount to a mere monologue that isolates and alienates us from God, our Lawgiver. Therefore, one's judgment doesn't become true by the mere fact that it has its origin in conscience, because a conscience needs to be truthfully formed first so as to echo the natural law. As Pope John Paul II put it in *Veritatis Splendor*, "The relationship between man's freedom and God's law is most deeply lived out in the 'heart' of the person, in his moral conscience" (54).

Seen from this perspective, it is hopefully much easier to see how those who started and led the Inquisitions could think their actions were highly justified. They were protecting the Church from divisions and heresies. They were making sure everyone's "compass" was accurate, without any deviations. Heresy may not always be detected by each individual's personal compass because of interference that needs to be corrected for. Therefore, it needs the compass of something like the Inquisition—guided by safe procedures, qualified inquisitors, and internal checks—which, unfortunately, does not always exclude individual errors.

The modern mindset finds it difficult to understand this institution, because many have, to no small extent, lost sight of two facts. On the one hand they have ceased to grasp religious belief as something objective, as a gift from God, and therefore outside the realm of free private judgment. On the other hand, they no longer see in the Church a society perfect and sovereign, based substantially on a pure and authentic Revelation, whose primary duty naturally must be to retain untarnished this original deposit of the Faith. Yet, before the religious revolution of the 16th century, this view was still common to all Christians—the view that orthodoxy should be maintained at any cost seemed self-evident.

How to Deal with Heresy

The Apostles were deeply imbued with the conviction that they must transmit the deposit of the Faith to posterity undefiled, and that any teaching at variance with their own would be a culpable offense. Nevertheless, St. Paul did not, in the case of the heretics Alexander and Hymeneus, go back to the Old Covenant penalties of death or scourging (Deuteronomy 13:6ff; 17:1ff); instead, he deemed exclusion from the communion of the Church sufficient (1 Timothy 1:20; Titus 3:10).

Jesus had ordained that the weed should be allowed to grow together with the wheat until the day of the harvest, lest the wheat be uprooted with the weed; those who are weed today might be converted tomorrow, and turn into wheat; let them therefore live, and let mere excommunication suffice. This tradition remained alive for a while. When Lucius Lactantius, who was yet suffering under the scourge of bloody persecutions, wrote his *Divinae Institutiones* in 308 (V:20), he still defended the most absolute freedom of religion:

Religion being a matter of the will, it cannot be forced on anyone; in this matter it is better to employ words than blows. Of what use is cruelty? What has the rack to do with piety? Surely there is no connection between truth and violence, between justice and cruelty. . . . It is true that nothing is so important as religion, and one must defend it at any cost. . . . It is true that it must be protected, but by dying for it, not by killing others; by long-suffering, not by violence; by faith, not by crime. If you attempt to defend religion with bloodshed and torture, what you do is not defense, but desecration and insult. For nothing is so intrinsically a matter of free will as religion.

The Christian teachers of the first three centuries insisted, as was natural to them, on complete religious liberty; furthermore, they not only urged the principle that religion could not be forced on others—a principle always adhered to by the Church in her dealings with the unbaptized—but, when comparing the Mosaic Law and the Christian religion, they taught that the latter was satisfied with a spiritual punishment of heretics (i.e., with excommunication), while Judaism necessarily proceeded against its dissidents with torture and death. Again, even the Inquisition did not force the Catholic religion on anyone, but only on members of the Catholic Church.

When the Church was confronted with the heresy of Manichaeism, she refused again to invoke civil power against it; indeed, St. Augustine, the great Bishop of Hippo, explicitly rejected the use of force. He sought their return only through public and private acts of submission, and his efforts seem to have met with success. Nevertheless, his response to heresy sometimes looks ambiguous, depending on whom he is addressing. In his correspondence with State officials, he dwells on Christian charity and toleration, and represents the heretics as straying lambs, to be sought out and perhaps, if recalcitrant, chastised with rods and frightened with threats of severity but not to be driven back to the fold by means of rack and sword. On the other hand, in his writings against the heretics, he upholds the rights of the State; sometimes, he says, a salutary severity would be to the interest of the erring ones themselves and likewise protective of true believers and the community at large.

Given this ambiguity, how would later centuries deal with heresy?

With the victory of Constantine in the second decade of the Fourth Century, followed by the conversion of most of the Roman Empire by the end of the century, Christianity became the Faith of the Empire. While this ended the age of martyrdom under intermittent Roman persecution, it created its own difficulties. Most prominent was the relationship of the Church—particularly Church authority—to the Christian emperors. It was a problem that, in certain respects, would plague Church relationships with government until the dramatic changes of the late 19th century and early 20th century. Government wanted to control the Church within its borders, seeing the Faith as inextricably linked to societal stability, identity, and as foundational to royal power. At the same time, the Church wanted to be seen as separate from this "City of Man," while also seeing in the secular arm the means to assure orthodox belief.

The imperial successors of Constantine soon began to see themselves as masters of the temporal and material conditions of the Church. They were convinced that the first concern of imperial authority was the protection of religion and so, with terrible regularity, issued many penal edicts against heretics. In the space of 57 years, 68 enactments were thus promulgated. But although they believed that one of the chief duties of an imperial ruler was to place his sword at the service of the Church and orthodoxy, the principal teachers of the Church held back for centuries from accepting the practice of the civil rulers in these matters; they shrank particularly from such stern measures against heresy as punishment, which they deemed inconsistent with the spirit of Christianity. St. Hilary of Poitiers in particular protested vigorously against any use of force in the province of religion, whether for the spread of Christianity or for preservation of the Faith.

But in the Middle Ages, the welfare of the Commonwealth came to be closely bound up with the cause of religious unity. The people accused the clergy of being too lenient in pursuing heretics. In 1144, Bishop Adalerbo II of Liège hoped to bring some imprisoned Catharists to better knowledge through the grace of God, but the people, less indulgent, assailed the unhappy creatures; it was only with the greatest trouble that the bishop could succeed in rescuing some of them from death by fire. A similar drama was enacted about the same time at Cologne. While the archbishop and the priests earnestly sought to lead the misguided back into the Church, the latter were violently taken by the mob from the custody of the clergy and burned at the stake.

St. Bernard of Clairvaux disagreed so much with the methods of the people of Cologne that he laid down the following axiom: "By persuasion, not by violence, are men to be won to the Faith." The obstinate were to be excommunicated, and if necessary kept in confinement for the safety of others The synods of that period employed substantially the same terms, e.g., the synod at Reims in 1049 under Pope Leo IX, that at Toulouse in 1119, at which Pope Callixtus II presided, and finally the Lateran Council of 1139.

It was the uncontrollable fanaticism of local mobs of heresy hunters, the indifference of certain churchmen, and the violence of secular courts that led to a determined effort by the papacy to exercise greater control over the determination and prosecution of heresy. One of the outcomes was that heresy could lead to a death penalty, usually that of being burnt at the stake. It is important to notice that death was not an exclusively Catholic punishment. It is well known that belief in the justice of punishing heresy with death was so common among the sixteenth century reformers—Luther, Zwingli, Calvin, and their adherents—that we may say their toleration began where their power ended. To the great humiliation of the Protestant churches, religious intolerance and even persecution unto death were continued long after the Reformation. In Geneva, severe persecution was put into practice by State and Church, including the use of torture and even the admission of the testimony of children against their parents—all of this was done with the sanction of John Calvin. Conservative estimates indicate that thousands of English and Irish Catholics were put to death—many by being hanged, drawn, and quartered—for practicing the Catholic Faith and refusing to become Protestant. An even greater number were forced to flee to the Continent for their safety. Apparently both sides easily understood the Bible to require the use of penal sanctions to root out false religion from Christian society.

Heresy is a very common Christian concern and should not be branded as peculiar to Catholicism. To blame Catholics for "the

Inquisition" is an unfair statement. The question does remain, though, if all those directing the inquisitions did a perfect job. They certainly did not. Does this put a blemish on the Church's authority? In a sense, it does; in another sense, it does not.

Let me explain. In his dispute with the Donatists, St. Augustine addressed a similar issue. Donatism was the heresy that the effectiveness of the sacraments depends on the moral character of the minister. In other words, if a minister involved in a serious enough sin were to baptize a person, that baptism would be considered invalid. St. Augustine pointed out that the problem with Donatism is that no person is morally pure. The administration of sacraments does not cease to be efficacious when the sinfulness of the minister is in question—say, of someone like Graham Greene's "whiskey priest." God is the one who works in and through them, and God is not restricted by the moral state of the administrant. The point is that the Church is holy, but her members are not. She is not holy because of the people who bear various titles—it is her message that makes her holy. Something similar can be said about the Inquisition: Even though the inquisitors cannot possibly be holy or morally pure, the Church remains holy, letting God work through her members, in spite of their imperfection.

Let us conclude this chapter by stating very clearly that the Inquisition never imposed a religion on anyone. What it does enforce is that those who follow the Catholic religion stay within the doctrinal boundaries of their Catholic faith, in respect for the deposit of faith that the Church has received from the Apostles.

Myth 4
Galileo Muzzled by the Church

A sk any group of people how the Catholic Church deals with science, and you can almost bank on it that some of them will bring up the Galileo case to prove the anti-science position of the Church. Why? It is the only instance that critics or enemies of the Catholic Church can quote in the history of science. It is the "one stock argument," in the words of John Henry Cardinal Newman, constantly trotted out against the Church to prove that science and Catholic dogma are each other's enemies.

We all seem to know, for example, that the astronomer Galileo was tortured and imprisoned for years by the Roman Inquisition. He then recanted his scientific theory on the rotation of the earth around the sun, but bravely muttered aloud as he left the trial chamber, "And yet it does move." To many, Galileo was martyred by the Catholic Church for his faith in science.

The historical reality, however, is that Galileo never said "And yet it moves" as he rose from his knees after renouncing Copernicanism—this defiant quote was a fabrication created after his death. There is no record of any such thing. And no, he was never tortured, nor was he condemned and burned at the stake. Instead, he lived in comfort at the Florentine embassy during his trial. Hardly, one could say, a real martyr.

Galileo's run-in with the Catholic Church is certainly one of the best-known episodes in the history of science. Though conventional wisdom dictates that the controversy was simply a clash between Galileo's heliocentric theory and the traditional view that the Sun revolved around Earth, there was a lot more going on than simply a disagreement about astronomy. If he was accused of heresy, it was not the "heresy" of heliocentrism, like so many claim, but the heresy of his theological escapades. It is time to separate fiction from non-fiction.

The Science of Galileo

The Good Part

To begin with, the problem in the Galileo conflict was not a flat earth. Pythagoras and others had already assumed that the earth was a sphere. Although St. Basil the Great declared it "a matter of no interest to us whether the earth is a sphere or a cylinder or a disk, or concave in the middle like a fan," influential Christian thinkers such as St. Clement, Origen, St. Ambrose, St. Augustine, and St. Thomas Aquinas all accepted the earth was a globe. Columbus faced trouble going west not because his sailors thought they would sail off the edge of the world but because they rightly thought that the distance between Europe and the East Indies was much greater than Columbus did.

A more serious problem, however, was the heliocentric model (with the sun in the center) versus the old geocentric model (with the earth in the center). The popular view is that it was Copernicus who "discovered" that the earth revolves around the sun. Actually, the notion of a revolving earth is at least as old as the ancient Greeks. But the geocentric theory, endorsed by Aristotle and given mathematical plausibility by Ptolemy, was the prevailing model until Copernicus. Because he had tried to generate results in a deductive fashion, Aristotle had made them seem a logical necessity.

But the Church had not wholeheartedly embraced Aristotle's geocentric view. St. Thomas Aquinas, for instance, astutely noticed that the visible motions of the celestial bodies "are produced either by the motion of the object seen or by the motion of the observer . . . it makes no difference which one is moving." In other words, the sun could be moving, or we could be moving. Elsewhere, Aquinas states, "The suppositions that these men [Ptolemaic astronomers] have invented need not necessarily be true: for perhaps, while they *save the appearances* under these suppositions, they might not be true. For maybe the phenomena of the stars can be explained by some other schema not yet discovered by men" (italics mine). Apparently, Aquinas understood that the Ptolemaic theory was just that, a theory, and that there could be other theories. God created the world in the way he wished to, not the way Aristotle said he had to.

Nicholas Copernicus (1473–1543) was the first one after the Middle Ages to publish the idea of a heliocentric model, suggesting that the earth orbited the sun. He was a Polish astronomer—probably not a priest as often claimed, but definitely a canon and a Third Order or Secular Dominican. In 1543, he published *On the Revolution of the Celestial Orbs*, in which he supported heliocentricity. The Aristotelian-Ptolemaic theory dominant at the time was such a complex system, with its numerous epicycles, that nobody believed that it corresponded to the physical reality of the universe. It accounted for observations and could be used in predicting the position of heavenly bodies, so it was nothing more than a mathematical model—in other words, it "saved the appearances" (a notion inherited from the ancient Greeks). According to this view, the heliocentric theory, or any physical theory for that matter, was nothing more than a convenient ordering of data with no intrinsic bearing on reality. Copernicus, though, found this practice of "saving appearances" to be "a confession of ignorance and confusion," and instead advocated scientific realism for his system.

Copernicus, a Catholic in good standing, published his book at the urging of two eminent prelates and dedicated it to Pope Paul III, who received it cordially. The almost universal belief that the purpose of science was not to give a final account of reality, but merely to "save appearances," accounts for how lightly the Church hierarchy initially received Copernicus's theory. The real fear of some churchmen was not a new theory of the nature of celestial movements, but a new theory about reality and truth—namely, that, if a hypothesis saves all the appearances, it must also be identical with truth. That Copernicus actually believed the heliocentric model to be a true description of *reality* went largely unnoticed.

How could this revolutionary twist of Copernicus's claim remain unnoticed? Copernicus had asked Andreas Osiander, a Lutheran clergyman, to write a preface to the book, because he knew that it would be attacked by Protestants (which it was) for its opposition to Scripture. Osiander also knew that Luther and Melanchthon violently opposed any suggestions that the earth revolved around the sun. So he wrote an unsigned preface, which everyone took to be from Copernicus himself, presenting the heliocentrism theory as a mere *hypothesis* for charting the movements of the planets in a simpler manner than the burdensome Ptolemaic system. The Catholic Church gave no censure to Copernicus, and the book was well-received by the Jesuit astronomers of the time.

Such was the scientific mindset of Europe when Galileo burst on the scene in 1610 with his startling telescopic discoveries. Up to that point, the forty-six-year-old Galileo had been interested mainly in physics and mathematics, not astronomy. His most famous accomplishment had been the formulation of the laws of falling bodies. Galileo was a gifted thinker, and when he heard about the invention of the telescope in Holland—called a spyglass—he immediately built one for himself, characteristically taking full credit for the invention.

Looking through his new "spyglass," he made some discoveries which shook the foundations of the Aristotelian cosmos. First, he saw that the moon was not a perfect sphere, but pocked with mountains and valleys like the earth. Second, he saw spots on the Sun, which revealed the rotation of the Sun. Third, and more astonishing, he discovered that Jupiter had at least four satellites—which are still called the Galilean moons: Io, Europa, Ganymede, and Callisto. No longer could it be said that heavenly bodies revolve only around the earth. Then he observed the phases of Venus, the only explanation of which is that Venus moves around the sun and not the earth.

Did Galileo prove heliocentricity? Many people wrongly believe he did. He could not answer the strongest argument against it, which had been made nearly two thousand years earlier by Aristotle himself. If the earth did orbit the sun, the philosopher wrote, then stellar parallaxes would be observable in the sky. In other words, there would be a shift in position of a star observed from the earth on one side of the sun, and then six months later from the other side. However, given the technology of Galileo's time, no such shifts in their positions could possibly be observed. It would require more sensitive measuring equipment than was available in Galileo's day to document the existence of these shifts, given the stars' great distance. This lack of evidence was one of the main reasons why the respected astronomer Tycho Brahe had refused to adopt fully Copernicus. The case was not decided until 1838, when Friedrich Bessel succeeded in determining the parallax of star 61 Cygni.

Galileo could not define what "proof" meant in astronomy, but he had no need to do so. The heliocentric model had been corroborated by the discovery of the phases of Venus by the Jesuit mathematicians of the Collegio Romano in 1611. Not only had they made their findings quite public during an elaborate celebration of Galileo at the Collegio in the spring of 1611, but their report had entered the Church's record by virtue of having been sent to the head of the Holy Office. As he would do more often, Galileo was able to use the Church's authority as a supplement for a notion of proof he badly needed but whose articulation and legitimation he could only defer.

It is fair to say that heliocentrism, as proposed by Galileo, and by Copernicus before him, was more of a vision than an established fact. Galileo was well aware of his lack of evidence; he was even of the opinion that no experiment performed on the earth could serve as a proof of its parallax motion (although, two centuries later, Léon Foucault would prove him wrong). But in spite of this lack of evidence, Galileo deserves praise for his scientific achievements.

The Not-So-Good Part

Did the astronomer Galileo also make mistakes? Of course, he did—every scientist does—and Galileo was no exception. When in 1632 Galileo published—with papal permission—a book called *Dialogue Concerning the Two Chief World Systems* (written in Italian for a change), he did support the Copernicus model, but he refused to adopt Kepler's model, which would ultimately become the winner.

Johannes Kepler had improved the Copernican system by replacing circular orbits with *elliptical* orbits. As his writings make clear, Kepler had been inspired by his religious faith to figure out a perfect system, because he knew God would not tolerate the inaccuracy that still plagued the older models. Yet, Kepler was persecuted by the Protestant faculty at Tübingen and took refuge with the Jesuits in 1596. Luther had already dismissed Copernicus as "that fool," and Melancthon had condemned Copernicanism as "dishonest" and "pernicious."

It is fair to say that Galileo's defense of the heliocentric plan did not depend on whether the orbits were circular or elliptical. Galileo refused to adopt Kepler's system, because his Pythagorean philosophy forced him to stick with "perfect" circles rather than "imperfect" ellipses, making him the advocate of a soon outdated view—circular motions of a spherical earth. In that sense, his heliocentric model was in essence not any better than Ptolemy's geocentric one. It is true that, until Tycho Brahe, there were not good enough observations to detect the ellipticity of Mars's orbit. Besides, Galileo was not particularly interested in the fine details of celestial mechanics. All that mattered to him was defending heliocentrism—which would be the same anyway, whether the orbits were circular or elliptical.

Nevertheless, Galileo continued his refusal to listen to Kepler, who had the data and formulated what we now call Kepler's laws of planetary motion—but Galileo would not listen to anyone it seems. Galileo's belligerence probably had much to do with the fact that he knew there was no direct proof of heliocentrism. Nevertheless, Galileo kept insisting, despite the discoveries of Kepler, that the planets orbit the sun in perfect circles—basically an Aristotelian conviction. He even launched his campaign with a series of pamphlets and letters which were circulated all over Europe.

When forced to prove his heliocentrism, he kept hinting that he had worked out such a proof, based on the tides. It was presented by Galileo in the fourth part of the *Dialogue*. His theory of the tides purported to show that the tides are caused by the rotation of the earth. Galileo maintained the tides were caused by the sloshing back and forth of water in the seas as a point on the Earth's surface sped up and slowed down because of the Earth's rotation on its axis and revolution around the Sun. If this theory were correct, there would be only one high tide per day, but even Galileo knew of this inadequacy because there are two daily high tides at Venice instead of one, about twelve hours apart. Galileo dismissed this anomaly as the result of several secondary causes including the shape of the sea, its depth, and other factors.

Within a year, it was stated in print that Galileo's proof was based on a confusion between two coordinate systems, one pivoted on the earth's center and the other on a point of its surface. Besides, after claiming that the tides were caused by the earth's rotation, Galileo then used that false claim to argue for the Copernican thesis that the earth is in motion—and not the heavens. We must come to the conclusion that Galileo was the kind of visionary who at times could not see his own self-contradictions. But he was so determined to find a much-needed proof for his heliocentrism that he probably was blind for any inconsistencies—at least that was the impression of Albert Einstein.

Galileo also believed that the sun was not just the fixed center of the solar system but also the fixed center of the universe. We now know that the sun is not the center of the universe and that it does move—it simply orbits the center of the galaxy rather than the earth. So we must conclude that both Galileo and his opponents were partly right and partly wrong. Galileo was right in asserting the mobility of the earth and wrong in asserting the immobility of the sun. His opponents were right in asserting the mobility of the sun and wrong in asserting the immobility of the earth.

Then there was another important dissident regarding heliocentrism—one of the most prominent astronomers of the time, Tycho Brahe. Careful measurements of star diameters had showed that, were the Copernican system correct, stars would be enormous. By contrast, under a geocentric system, the sizes of celestial bodies would all fall into a consistent range. The moon would be the smallest celestial body, the sun the largest. The stars would be comparable to, but smaller than, the sun. Copernicans had little to which they might object. They resorted to justifying the absurdly large stars in their system by appealing to Divine Majesty and Omnipotence—an infinitely powerful God could easily make such giant stars. No wonder, then, that Galileo consistently refuses to mention the name of Tycho Brahe.

Along the way, Galileo picked some fights with a number of churchmen on peripheral matters—which helped to stack the deck against him. And, despite the warnings of his friends in Rome, he insisted on moving the debate onto theological grounds. When certain theologians objected that his theory seemed contrary to Scripture, he entered, with no expertise, into a theological discussion on the proper mode of interpreting Scripture. Unfortunately this intemperance in debate and its theological shift led finally to Galileo's "trial" and house arrest.

Galileo was a good scientist; he was also a dedicated Catholic—he did not deny the truths of the Catholic Faith—but he was extremely stubborn and, in some sense, a rascal, always ready for a fight with anyone, no matter whether they were astronomers or theologians. He felt he had the expertise to address all fields of knowledge, and he claimed more evidence for his heliocentric assertions than he actually had. Accordingly, he was more of an ideologist than a scientist.

Ironically, Galileo became more known for his not-so-impressive astronomical achievements than for his other scientific work. It was while he was under house arrest that he dedicated his time to one of his finest books, *Two New Sciences*. In this book, he summarized work he had done some forty years earlier, on the two sciences now called kinematics and strength of materials. This book was later highly praised by Albert Einstein, who called Galileo the "father of modern physics." Galileo was one of the first modern thinkers to clearly state that the laws of nature are mathematical. Galileo also put forward the basic principle of relativity, that the laws of physics are the same in any system that is moving at a constant speed in a straight line, regardless of its particular speed or direction. Hence, there is no absolute motion or absolute rest. This principle provided the basic framework for Newton's laws of motion and is central to Einstein's special theory of relativity.

Support of the Church

What Galileo Gained

In general, the response to Galileo's claims ranged from enthusiastic to downright hostile. The leading Jesuit astronomer of the day, Christopher Clavius, was skeptical at first; but once the Roman College acquired an improved telescope, he saw for himself that Galileo was right about Jupiter's moons, and the Jesuit astronomers soon confirmed the phases of Venus. However, these men were not ready to jump on the heliocentric bandwagon immediately; they adopted as a halfway house the system of Tycho Brahe, which had all the planets except the earth orbiting the sun. This system accounted quite satisfactorily for all of Galileo's discoveries. Was it just a compromise? No, it was a perfect fit for all the data available at the time—at least as perfect as Galileo's alternative.

Still, Galileo was the man of the hour, with a knack for maintaining image. In 1611, he made a victorious visit to Rome, where he was honored by cardinals and granted a private audience by Pope Paul V, who assured him of his support and good will. He enjoyed a long audience with the pope and with the Jesuits of the Roman College. Those who were present included Fr. Christoph Grienberger, who had invented a telescope which rotated on an axis parallel to the Earth's, and Fr. Clavius, one of the great mathematicians of the day who had helped to develop the Gregorian calendar. Interestingly enough, Copernican theories had been used to reform the calendar in 1582. Everything was going well for Galileo in Rome.

In fact, most Jesuit astronomers agreed with the new astronomy. And they were important allies; even Galileo himself regarded the Jesuits of the Roman College, who were the leading astronomers of the day, as what he called, in his own words, "modern-minded humanists, friends of science and discovery." Indeed, there are some thirty craters on the moon named after Jesuit astronomers.

Like the Jesuit astronomers, many theologians at the time were "modern-minded" as well. One of the main players in the upcoming debate was the Jesuit Cardinal St. Robert Bellarmine, who made a distinction between two different types of astronomy (e.g., in his letter of April 12, 1615 to Foscarini). He recognized, on the one hand, a mathematical astronomy which tries to come up with systems that do justice to the phenomena—thus "saving appearances." On the other hand, he singled out a physical astronomy that attempts to ascertain which mathematical system of the many available actually applies to the physical structure of the heavens. Later on, the 20th century physicist Pierre Duhem suggested that in one respect, at least, Bellarmine had shown himself a better scientist than Galileo by disallowing the possibility of a "strict proof of the earth's motion," on the grounds that an astronomical theory merely "saves the appearances" without necessarily revealing what "really happens."

What Bellarmine essentially pointed out was that it was perfectly acceptable to maintain Copernicanism as a working hypothesis; but only if there were "real proof" that the earth does circle around the sun, "then we should have to proceed with great circumspection in explaining passages of Scripture which appear to teach the contrary." The cardinal's reasoning was logical and perfectly correct: the same set of data may be consistent with different (mathematical) hypotheses, so it requires an extra step to figure out which hypothesis is actually true. This was perfectly in line with Aquinas's statement that "maybe the phenomena of the stars can be explained by some other schema not yet discovered by men." Bellarmine deemed it harmless to claim that the sun is in the center if one uses a mathematical approach. But such claim, he said, would require much more confirming evidence, if one were to claim this to be actually the case in a physical sense.

And that was the heart of problem—the need for more evidence. Cardinal Bellarmine, in effect, challenged Galileo to prove his theory or stop pestering the Church. He wrote in his letter to Foscarini,

> if there were a true demonstration that . . . the sun did not go around the earth but the earth went around the sun, then it would be necessary to use careful consideration in explaining the Scriptures that seemed contrary.

All that St. Bellarmine required was more and stronger scientific evidence in favor of heliocentrism before the interpretation of Scripture should be questioned. Galileo's response, as we saw earlier, was to produce his theory of the tides, which purported to show that the tides are caused by the rotation of the earth. Even some of Galileo's friends could see that this was patent nonsense. So the scientific case was far from settled—no matter what some claim now, seen in retrospect.

What Galileo Lost

After his glorious visit to Rome in 1611, Galileo returned to Florence, where he might have been expected to continue his scientific research. Instead, he became obsessed with converting public opinion to the Copernican system. He was an early instance of that very modern type: the cultural and political scientist. All of Europe, starting with the Church, had to buy into the heliocentric model of

Copernicus. Galileo was a passionately driven man with a new, sacred mission.

Initially, Galileo had powerful friends among Cardinals, Jesuits, even popes. However, in time, he would lose their support—not only because of scientific disputes, but also because of the frequency and acidity of Galileo's attacks. All these factors played an important role in causing many Jesuits to withdraw their much-needed support of Galileo. What irked Church officials was not so much what Galileo was saying, but how he was saying it.

It was during this time that Galileo became highly embroiled in a controversy with the eminent Jesuit mathematician and astronomer Horazio Grassi over the nature of comets. Fr. Grassi had come to the conclusion that the comet was a fiery body which had moved along a segment of a great circle at a constant distance from the earth, and since it moved in the sky more slowly than the moon, it must be farther away than the moon. Galileo criticized this view by declaring comets mere optical effects caused by vapors rising from the earth. Although we now know that Galileo was on the wrong side of the argument, his irony and wit took their toll on his opponent. Galileo had previously already gotten into a dispute with another Jesuit, Fr. Christopher Scheiner, over the priority of the discovery of sunspots. (Scholars now believe that neither man was the first.) Undoubtedly, these controversies helped cement the Jesuits' opposition to Galileo, an opposition that carried no small weight in Rome.

But Galileo loved controversies. The Church had no objection to the use of the Copernican system as a hypothesis whose truth was not yet established. Galileo, however, believed his model to be literally true even though he lacked adequate evidence to support the physical truth of his theory at the time. But Galileo refused to present his theory as only a hypothesis and insisted writing about it as proven truth. He even had a series of pamphlets and letters circulate all over Europe. In short, he refused to compromise.

As a matter of fact, Galileo was intent on ramming Copernicus down the throat of Christendom. The irony is that when he started his campaign, he enjoyed almost universal good will among the Catholic hierarchy. But he managed to alienate almost everybody with his caustic manner and aggressive tactics. His position gave the

Church authorities no room to maneuver: they either had to accept Copernicanism as a fact and reinterpret the Scriptures accordingly, or they had to condemn it. He refused the reasonable third alternative which the Church offered him: that Copernicanism might be considered only a hypothesis, one even superior to the Ptolemaic system, until further proof could be adduced. It is ironic when you realize that Copernicanism with its circular orbits would soon be obsolete. The Church had it right.

In December of 1613, a key event took place, setting events in motion that ultimately led to Galileo's trial. Benedetto Castelli, a Benedictine monk, professor of physics at Pisa, and a disciple of Galileo, had breakfast with the Grand Duke and Duchess of Tuscany, Galileo's patrons. They asked Castelli to explain the recent astronomical discoveries. This led naturally to a discussion of the heliocentric theory. Cosimo Boscaglia, a professor of philosophy also at Pisa, began to argue against the earth's motion, saying it was against Scripture. The Grand Duchess, a pious and devout lady, was concerned about these objections, and Castelli answered as best as he could. Later when he wrote to Galileo telling him of the incident, Galileo replied in a letter and laid out some of his own ideas on scriptural interpretation.

In this famous *Letter to Castelli* in 1613, Galileo did accept the inerrancy of Scripture; but he was also mindful of Cardinal Baronius's quip that the Bible "is intended to teach us how to go to heaven, not how the heavens go"—a remark that Baronius probably had made in conversation with Galileo. And Galileo pointed out correctly that both St. Augustine and St. Thomas Aquinas taught that the sacred writers in no way meant to teach a system of astronomy. Here is part of the letter:

> I think that in disputes about natural phenomena one must begin not with the authority of scriptural passages but with sensory experience and necessary demonstrations. . . . I do not think that one has to believe that the same God who has given us senses, language, and intellect would want to set aside the use of these and give us by other means the information we can acquire with them, so that we would deny our senses and reason even in the case of those physical conclusions which are placed before our eyes and

intellect by our sensory experiences or by necessary demonstration.

When Galileo heard that various rumors and errors about him were being spread, he decided to extend this letter and publish it. This resulted in his letter to the Grand Duchess Christina, entitled "Concerning the Use of Biblical Quotations in Matters of Science." Although he wrote this essay in order to defend himself against allegations of heresy, the effect of publishing it was to irritate the Church authorities, who up to this point had not been inclined to get involved in the matter. In their view, Galileo was a mere mathematician, unqualified to speak about matters of theology, and it was taken as presumptuous of him to do so. Cardinal Robert Bellarmine, at that time the Church's chief theologian, sent signals through the Tuscan ambassador to the Vatican and other friends of Galileo, that Galileo would be safe from the Inquisition provided that he treated the Copernican theory only as a hypothesis and not as physically true, and that he did not try to reconcile Scripture with his unproven theory. Galileo was unwilling to accept this advice, being convinced of the physical reality of the Copernican model, and also unwilling to be quiet. He took on a fight.

In February of 1615, Nicolò Lorini, a Dominican preacher and professor of history at Florence, filed a complaint against Galileo with the Roman Inquisition, giving them an insidiously altered copy of Galileo's letter to Castelli. For instance, Galileo wrote, "There are in Scripture words which, taken in the strict literal meaning, look as if they differed from the truth." Lorini altered this to read, "which are false in the literal meaning." Galileo wrote, "Scripture has not abstained from somewhat concealing its most essential dogmas; thus attributing to God himself properties contrary to and very far from his essence." Lorini changed "concealing" to "perverting." The inquisitors were very suspicious of Lorini's motives, and quietly asked Castelli for a correct copy of the letter, but it seems that for various reasons they never received one. Nevertheless, no conclusive evidence was found against Galileo at this time. The Consulter of the Inquisition found no serious objections to the letter, and the case was dismissed.

However, the *Letter to Castelli* was on the files of the Inquisition, and Rome was buzzing with rumors that the Church was going to condemn both Galileo and Copernicanism. Galileo's friends in the hierarchy, including Cardinal Barberini, the future Urban VIII, warned him not to force the issue. But Galileo only intensified his campaign to get the Church to accept Copernicanism as an irrefutable truth. Ironically, he wanted the Church to back his *scientific* claims.

Not only had Galileo in this letter expressed his scientific views supporting Copernicus, but he had also addressed related biblical views. This was considered by some as another (perhaps heretical?) Scripture interpretation by a lay person in an era of rampant lay interpretation of Scripture by many Protestant reformers. What shocked them was that Galileo had taken it upon himself to interpret Scripture according to his private insights. We have to realize that at the time of Galileo's first "trial," there was precious little elasticity in Catholic biblical theology, because the Church had just been through the bruising battles of the Reformation. One of the chief quarrels with the Protestants was over the private interpretation of Scripture—and here was another private interpretation. Catholic theologians were in no mood to entertain semi-theological injunctions from a lay person like Galileo. His friend Cardinal Dini warned him that he could write freely so long as he "kept out of the sacristy." But Galileo threw caution to the winds, and it was on this point—his apparent trespassing on theologians' territory—that his enemies were finally able to nail him.

The inquisitors were well aware that they were not competent to evaluate the scientific case. They followed proper procedure by requesting expert opinions on the matter. Perhaps if the scientific experts had been unanimous in their support of Copernicus, the theologians would have bowed to their authority. But the scientific community was divided on the subject too—the scientific case was still very controversial. And so the condemnation proceeded.

Although in February of 1615, Galileo had been exonerated, the Inquisition had decided to further consult its experts for an opinion on the status of Copernicanism. It was in 1616 that a team of eleven Roman Inquisition's consultants gave their assessment and "censured" Galileo. The most quoted part of this hastily written verdict is the statement that the heliocentric system of Nicolaus Copernicus was declared to be "foolish and absurd in philosophy" and "formally heretical." There has been ample discussion about the original punctuation between *philosophia* and *et formaliter haereticam*; it appears to be a comma with a somewhat elongated dot above it, suggesting a semicolon. If that is the case, then the verdict makes two separate declarations. It declares the theory untenable on a purely scientific basis, and then declares it also heretical in purely Scriptural terms. So the verdict did not—as many seem to assume—suppress a scientific idea, declaring it "foolish and absurd" only because it was religiously inconvenient. There was indeed much scientific evidence *against* the new theory, as we will soon discuss in more detail.

This was the first of two trials of the Roman Inquisition. The Inquisition Minutes of February 24, 1616, read as follows:

> His Holiness ordered the most Illustrious Lord Cardinal Bellarmine to call Galileo before himself and warn him to abandon these opinions; and if he should refuse to obey, the Father Commissary, in the presence of a notary and witnesses, is to issue him an injunction to abstain completely from teaching or defending this doctrine and opinion or from discussing it; and further, if he should not acquiesce, he is to be imprisoned.

On the following day, there was a meeting of the Cardinals of the Inquisition in which Cardinal Bellarmine would deliver this result to Galileo as instructed by Pope Paul V. According to the Special Injunction of that day (February 25, 1616), Cardinal Bellarmine did warn Galileo that the above-mentioned opinion was erroneous and that he should abandon it. Then the Cardinal

> ordered and enjoined the said Galileo, who was himself still present, to abandon completely the above-mentioned opinion that the sun stands still at the center of the world and the earth moves, and henceforth not to hold, teach, or defend it in any way whatever, either orally or in writing; otherwise the Holy Office would start proceedings against him. The same Galileo acquiesced in this injunction and promised to obey.

As a result of this censure, Galileo promised, under pain of further punishment, not to hold or publish Copernican theory as scientific fact, but only as an unproven theory or hypothesis. As a matter of pure science, the theory was indeed unproven at that time, by Galileo or by anyone, and was very much up in the air. It is not quite clear, though, what Cardinal Bellarmine actually said to Galileo—whether he ordered him not to "hold or defend" Copernicanism, or more strongly, not to "teach" Copernicanism in any way (the latter version, though, would not have been in line with Bellarmine's personal position).

In retrospect, we know that Galileo would have been right if he had talked in terms of "support"—rather than "proof"—for his theory. Science works with provisional confirmation, never definitive verification; there may be more and more supporting evidence, but never final proof. "Proven" in science usually means "accepted" until a new set of empirical data disprove what was previously considered "proven." The Victorian biologist Thomas Henry Huxley, who had no brief for the Catholic Church, once examined the case and concluded, "The Church had the best of it." The most striking point of the whole affair is that until Galileo rudely forced the issue into the realm of theology, the Church had served as a willing ombudsman for the new astronomy. It had encouraged the work of Copernicus and sheltered Kepler against the persecutions of the Calvinists. But now the real issues of the Galileo affair had gone far beyond the question of mere celestial mechanics.

This "crusade" would never have ended in the offices of the Inquisition had Galileo possessed a modicum of discretion, or, for that matter, charity. But he was not a tactful person; he loved to score off people and make them look ridiculous. And he would make no allowance for human nature, which does not easily chuck off an old cosmology to embrace a new one which seems to contradict sensory evidence, common sense, and tradition.

Then, in 1632, Galileo published *Dialogue of the Great World System*, in which he violated his 1616 agreement not to hold or defend Copernican theory as actual fact. The book was actually written at the urging of the Pope, now Urban VIII. It was an account of conversations between three participants—a Copernican scientist,

Salviati, an impartial and witty scholar named Sagredo, and a ponderous Aristotelian named Simplicio, who employed stock arguments in support of geocentricity, and was depicted in the book as being an intellectually inept fool. Simplicio's arguments were systematically refuted and ridiculed by the other two characters with "unassailable proof" for the Copernican theory, which reduces Simplicio to a baffled rage, and makes the author's position unambiguously clear. Galileo also further alienated the Jesuits by attacking one of their astronomers in the book. All of this eventually led to a new trial and his being sentenced to abjure his "heresy" (although it should be noted that three of the ten Cardinals who sat on that Commission refused to sign the judgment).

It should not surprise us that, by virtue of being in violation of his 1616 agreement with Rome, Galileo's new book was taken by the Church to be an open public challenge of their authority. So some months after the book's publication, Pope Urban VIII banned its sale and had its text submitted for examination by a special commission. Anyone reading it could tell that this was not an even-handed presentation of the evidence for and against each of the two theories, but a blast intended to destroy the Ptolemaic position and establish the Copernican one. The pope, feeling betrayed, was furious with Galileo. The book that Galileo had produced was very different from the one he had expected and would have approved. He had thought it would give much more weight to the uncertainties and doubts on both sides of the question. In the meantime, the pope learned of the Inquisition's minutes recording the special injunction to Galileo not to "hold, teach, or defend" the theory—an injunction about which Galileo had never informed him.

With the loss of many of his defenders in Rome because of his new book, Galileo was ordered to stand trial again in 1633, in violation of the 1616 condemnation, since

> it was decided at the Holy Congregation ... on 25 Feb 1616 that
> ... the Holy Office would give you an injunction to abandon this
> doctrine, not to teach it to others, not to defend it, and not to treat
> of it; and that if you did not acquiesce in this injunction, you
> should be imprisoned.

It is worth noting that the substance of the trial of 1633 was the question as to whether he had violated the decree issued in 1616, and no longer the question of the truth of Copernicanism itself. That latter issue was considered to have been settled in the first proceeding, and was not revisited. The issue at hand, and for which he was ultimately sentenced was not Galileo's science; it was the violation of his earlier agreement. Let us also make very clear that his "heresy" was not the earth moving around the sun, as many nowadays claim it was. The Church and her Inquisition do not deal with disputes in science but only with controversies in theology. And that's where Galileo went wrong, venturing into religious territory and claiming theological expertise in scriptural interpretations—especially at a time when many "private" interpretations of the Bible were abounding.

Not only was Galileo sentenced to abjure his heresy, but also to keep silent on the subject—and that for the rest of his life. After a period with the friendly Ascanio Piccolomini, the Archbishop of Siena, Galileo was allowed to return to his villa at Arcetri near Florence in 1634, where he spent the remainder of his life under house arrest. As the Harvard mathematician and philosopher Alfred North Whitehead put it, "In a generation which saw the Thirty Year's War and remembered Alva in the Netherlands, the worst that happened to men of science was that Galileo suffered an honorable detention and a mild reproof, before dying peacefully in his bed."

It appears that Galileo's temperament made him not the ideal diplomat; he seems to have enjoyed a good fight, and the more he was pressed, the more belligerent he would become. He defended his theory with passion and attacked foes with dominating, forceful, and even insulting sarcasm, which began to make him some serious and vengeful enemies—in science, in academia, and in the Church. His enemies accused him of ramming Copernicus down the throat of Christianity without sufficient scientific evidence, and even by using semi-theological arguments.

In those days, those who argued a new *scientific* theory would get the Church's attention, if only because so many high-ranking churchmen were also men of science, so the argument would be more or less on equal footing. But if someone ventured to argue a new *scriptural* interpretation, one immediately got the whole Church on her feet and antagonistic, and the argument would not stand on more or less equal footing. Theologians were not prepared to entertain the heliocentric theory based on a layman's interpretation of Scripture. Yet Galileo insisted on moving the debate into the theological arena. Galileo fell into the same error as his opponents: his philosophy affected the way he read the Bible. There is little question that if Galileo had kept the discussion within the accepted boundaries of astronomy and had not claimed physical truth for the heliocentric theory, the issue would not have escalated to the point it did.

As an interesting side note, both Luther and Calvin publicly condemned Galileo outright as a heretic, and would have had him burned at the stake if they could have gotten their hands on him. But while in Roman hands, Galileo was never tortured. Nor was he ever really imprisoned, in the normal sense of the term. While in Rome he was maintained in comfortable chambers with servants, and he spent the rest of his life under "house arrest" in his own home. This part of Church history may not be one of the nicest, but it was not as extreme and one-sided as portrayed in later versions of the conflict. It was a human drama played out by a cast of flawed and finite characters on both sides. It was a case of tragic mutual incomprehension.

What Kind of Conflict Was It?

How Obvious Were Galileo's Facts?

The conflict between Galileo and the Church is often portrayed as a battle in which the new science had to defeat the outdated philosophy of Aristotle with which the Church had aligned herself. In this distorted and fabricated view, the Church's favorite philosophy vehemently rejected the new facts that Galileo presented. Some said Galileo was not running up against Scripture but against Aristotelianism—assumptions such as mathematical perfection, an earth-centered universe with heavenly bodies moving in perfect circles. In this view, the Galileo case was heliocentrism versus Aristotelianism. The overall message is clear: The Church's influence on the world has been one of obscurantism and repression.

This caricature also made it into Bertold Brecht's playwright *Life of Galileo*. At some point, Brecht creates the following dialog between a philosopher, a mathematician, and Galileo himself:

—The Philosopher: "The worldview of the divine Aristotle . . . is a structure of such beauty and order that we should be very hesitant to disturb such harmony."

—Galileo: "But what if your majesty would now actually observe those impossible as well as unnecessary stars by use of this telescope?"

—The Mathematician: "One could be led to answer that your tube—when showing what cannot exist—would not be a very reliable tube, right?"

Brecht was sarcastic, of course, when writing this last line, but he did acknowledge that there was a wider battle going on here behind the scientific scenes. Was it the battle between an old philosophy and the new science? Or was it the power of formal sciences such as mathematics versus the power of empirical sciences—the latter depending on observational tools such as telescopes which must prove their reliability first? Interestingly enough, it was Galileo who was Aristotelian when he decided to stick with "perfect" circles rather than Kepler's "imperfect" ellipses, making him the advocate of a soon-to-be-outdated view—circular motions of a spherical earth.

The scientific case that Galileo was promoting was not as clear as many tend to think, because the astronomical "facts" were not very clear. First of all, when Galileo supported Copernicus's heliocentric model, he had to face some difficult "facts." If we go by Aristotelian theories of impulse and relative motion, the theory advanced by Galileo seems to be falsified by the "fact" that objects appear to fall vertically on earth rather than diagonally—the famous so-called "tower argument." Admittedly, the question of whether or not weights fall vertically was moot at that time because the measurements were not accurate enough to tell the difference.

Other "facts" seemed to confirm as well that the earth did not move, for if it did, the clouds would be left behind—a "fact" that Galileo himself had already remarked in a lecture of 1601. As Paul

Feyerabend, the late University of California at Berkeley philosopher of science, pointed out, one could state that Galileo's opponents kept closer to the "facts" than Galileo himself. One could certainly ask the question why the phenomena seen through a telescope should be called "facts," whereas the phenomena seen by the naked eye—sunrise at daybreak and sunset at the end of the day—are no longer considered "facts." From a common sense perspective, the sun does rise and set. What makes Galileo's observations more reliable than what everyone else sees in the sky?

Sensory evidence seemed to proclaim the stability of the earth as absolute verity. As Galileo put it a century later, Copernicus was faced with the prospect of committing a "rape of the senses." He could do so because, as Copernicus explicitly put it, the weightiest objection to heliocentrism, the Aristotelian doctrine of light and heavy, could be overcome with faith in the Creator's power and simplicity. His religious belief told him that God could move the earth if he so wished. Galileo saw Copernicus's greatness in his courage to ignore what his senses told him—even when it goes against the accepted "facts." Sometimes the witness of the senses also needs the eyes of the mind. As Francis Crick, one of the two scientists who discovered DNA, put it, "A theory that fits all the facts is bound to be wrong, as some of the facts will be wrong." Scientific information is very volatile by its very nature—it is always a work in progress.

There is an old cliché according to which science suddenly emerged when Galileo dropped weights from the Tower of Pisa and let balls roll down an inclined plane. But in the late 1930s, it was carefully pointed out by the French physicist Pierre Duhem and others that Galileo never dropped weights from any tower, and that he had derived the time-squared law of free fall long before he experimented with balls and inclined planes. For Galileo, it was enough to rely on "the eyes of the mind" in order to reach important scientific conclusions about the physical world—a valid move perhaps, but still controversial.

The observation that objects fall vertically on earth required a new interpretation to make it compatible with Copernican theory. Instead of taking the "facts" at face value, Galileo was able to make a conceptual change about the nature of impulse and relative motion, but before such theories were articulated, he had to use *ad hoc* methods and proceed counter-inductively—given the knowledge available at the time. Galileo himself had to commit "a rape of the senses," when he denied the rule of his eyes and all previous conclusions about moving objects.

This takes us to a related question: How reliable was Galileo's "tube" with which he created and confirmed his new "facts." His first telescope was based on an existing optical device in Holland, called spyglass (whereas modern refracting telescopes are based on a design proposed by Johannes Kepler in 1611 but first constructed by the Jesuit Christopher Scheiner, somewhere between 1613 and 1617). Galileo's kind of telescope fell out of favor with astronomers shortly after his death. Modern refracting telescopes dramatically improve the field of view. But Galileo still had to use a very primitive tool.

Then there is another problem. Just like students who use a microscope for the first time and see hardly anything, so astronomers must learn to use telescopes too. When Galileo demonstrated his simple telescope to a group of professors in Bologna in 1610, all admitted the instrument seemed to deceive; some fixed stars were actually seen double. Galileo had to concede in a letter to Johannes Kepler that many people were unable to see what they were "supposed" to see through his telescope. What we think the facts are may not actually be the facts.

Ironically, even Galileo himself would refer to comets as "optical illusions," rather than "facts," when he thought it would suit him well during his dispute over comets with the Jesuit astronomer Horazio Grassi—a dispute Galileo would eventually lose. It is also ironic that Grassi argued based on empirical observations and mathematics that comets are supra-lunar astronomical objects, whereas Galileo argued in true Aristotelian fashion that comets are sub-lunar meteorological phenomena, completely rejecting the mathematical arguments. We must also realize that there were no real experts in the field of optics at the time, except for Johannes Kepler and Horazio Grassi (and later on, scientists such as René Descartes, Isaac Newton, and Christiaan Huygens). So it is quite understandable that many scholars thought that all the things the new telescope showed them could only be "arti-facts," not "real-facts." The world of "facts" is certainly not a rock-solid world; the "facts" may be wrong. Was this a matter of philosophy versus science, of Aristotelianism versus Copernicanism? Upon investigation, it does not seem so.

The Galileo affair entered the mythological corpus of Western secularism as symbolizing the Church as being anti-science. His 1633 trial is most often portrayed as Galileo the scientist arguing the supremacy of *reason* versus the tribunal judges demanding that reason surrender to *faith*. But the trial was neither. Both Galileo, a firm and orthodox Catholic, and the tribunal judges shared a common view that science and the Bible could not stand in contradiction. If there appeared to be a contradiction, such a contradiction resulted from either weak science, or poor interpretation of Scripture. Seen in this context, the trial exhibited both faults. Galileo's technology was far too limited at the time to scientifically prove his assertion of the earth's rotation. At the same time, the tribunal judges were at fault for a literal interpretation of biblical passages and making scientific judgments that were never intended by the Scriptural authors.

We also should realize that both sides were in a process of shaping their own identity. In other words, what is "reason," and what is "faith"? What is science, and what is religion? The "case of Galileo" probably propelled this process. Nowadays we know the outcome, but that wasn't quite clear at the onset. Just think of the way astronomy had to distinguish itself from astrology, during that time, and how chemistry had to distance itself from alchemy. They all acquired more distinctiveness during the process.

All of this places Galileo's case in a much wider context. Ptolemy's methodizing of Aristotle to explain the motion of the stars was part of this academic baggage. Ptolemy's system made perfect empirical sense; by using it, ships had been able to navigate the seas, and astronomers had been able to predict eclipses. So why give up this time-honored system for a new, unproved cosmology which not only contradicted common sense, but also the apparent sense of Scripture? I do not think it unreasonable for churchmen like St.

Robert Bellarmine to have hesitated to reinterpret biblical verses along heliocentric lines until they were given more convincing evidence.

For one thing, Ptolemy and Copernicus did not exhaust all the range of possible cosmologies, as we discussed already. Since 1588 there was a well-known alternative to Copernicus and Ptolemy, and it was called Tycho. And, sadly for Galileo, Tycho's hybrid planetary model could easily account for the phases of Venus while keeping the earth at the center of the universe. Competent readers must have been flabbergasted to find no mention of Tycho in the "Letter to the Grand Duchess." Nor, for that matter, was Tycho mentioned in any of the texts Galileo wrote in the context of this dispute, or in his famous 1632 *Dialogue on the Two Chief World Systems*—the book that triggered the final trial of 1633. Galileo's erasure of Tycho was as stunning as it was mandatory. Tycho's model did not simply take the wind out of Galileo's alleged refutation of geocentrism, but, even more insidiously, it indicated that the "Book of Nature" (as it could be read at that time) had more than one reading, which is something Galileo would prefer to ignore.

Cardinal John Henry Newman, who was not one to think that secular truths are determined by ecclesiastical fiat, wrote concerning Galileo's "crusade" that

> had I been brought up in the belief of the immobility of the earth as though a dogma of Revelation, and had associated it in my mind with the incommunicable dignity of man among created beings, with the destinies of the human race, with the locality of purgatory and hell, and other Christian doctrines and then for the first time had heard of Galileo's thesis ... I should have been at once indignant at its presumptions and frightened at its speciousness, as I can never be, at any parallel novelties in other human sciences bearing on religion.

Faith and Reason Complement Each Other

The 1633 trial is most often portrayed as Galileo the scientist arguing the supremacy of *reason* and the tribunal judges demanding that reason surrender to *faith*. To the popular, biased mind, the Galileo affair is *prima facie* evidence that the free pursuit of truth became possible only after science "liberated" itself from the theological shackles of the Middle Ages. But that is a false contrast—faith and reason are not in a power battle; they are in fact best friends. As Pope Francis said in *Evangelii Gaudium* (#242): "Faith is not fearful of reason; on the contrary, it seeks and trusts reason." Then, quoting St. Thomas Aquinas, he adds that "the light of reason and the light of faith both come from God." So we do not have to make an exclusive choice here of either-or but instead we can embrace the synthesis of the "Grand And"—faith *and* reason.

As a matter of fact, it was faith rather than reason that had taught Copernicus that God, unlike the god of Plato, was an all-powerful being for whom nothing was easier than to have the earth move. A good Christian, Copernicus knew that no man—not even Aristotle—could dictate to his Creator. The simple system of heliocentrism had to match the data of observation. In the simple ordering of the cosmos, Copernicus saw a proof of the existence of God. He looked at the world as the product of a personal, rational Creator. Therefore, he could take the stable star providing safe navigation not as a sign of the stability of the sky but of the stability of God's Creation.

Because God is one, and man is made in the image of God, there can only be one truth, as St. Augustine had argued centuries ago. By St. Augustine's time, it had for seven hundred years been generally accepted in educated circles that the earth is spherical, whereas according to the Bible, the earth is a shallow disk floating on waters. To reconcile this difference, St. Augustine laid down an all-important rule in *De Genesi ad Litteram*: whenever something in the Bible about the physical world conflicts with what reason established on the same point, the Bible should be reinterpreted accordingly. When it comes to things physical, reason—or science, for that matter—is the final arbiter.

In this line of thought, there is a longstanding tradition in the Catholic Church of distinguishing between the *Book of Scripture* and the *Book of Nature*. Its origin can be found in these words of St. Augustine: "It is the divine page that you must listen to; it is the book of the universe that you must observe" (*Enarrationes in Psalmos*, 45, 7). This conviction was a belief shared in the past by many authors before Galileo: from the Apologetic Fathers to St. Basil; from St. Gregory of Nyssa to St. Augustine; from St. Albert the Great to St. Thomas Aquinas; from Roger Bacon to William of Ockham.

In his attempt to enter the domain of theology, Galileo resumed the use of the metaphor of the "two books" in order to defend the compatibility of his heliocentric system with Sacred Scripture. By positing the existence of two equally divine and true "books," Galileo was trying to claim that both theology and astronomy dealt with the same truth, but one that was written in two different books. In his "Letter to Maria Cristina of Lorraine" (1615), Galileo presented Nature and Scripture as two books proceeding from the same divine Word; therefore, the glory of God can also be known by means of the works that He has written in the "open book of heaven," as Galileo called it.

Why did Galileo revive and use the image of the Two Books? It was a smart move on his part, for several reasons. First, it placed astronomy not *under* theology, but *next* to theology, and thus turned a hierarchical relationship into a parallel one. In doing so, he also elevated the status of astronomy as a science that, like theology, dealt with the decoding of divine speech—the speech that authored both nature and Scripture. Galileo could then argue that when the reading of these two sacred books sent theology and astronomy on a collision course, such conflicts could no longer be resolved by considering which discipline was the most authoritative. As a consequence, without questioning the authority of theologians directly, he could still question their ultimate authority in conflicts between science and religion.

Galileo had a second reason for using the image of the Two Books. The authority of the Two Books is supposed to rest on the books themselves, not on those who read them, so clashes between theology and astronomy could only be solved through the books themselves, not through their "readers," the theologians and astronomers respectively. It was with this claim that Galileo changed the Book of Nature into a Trojan horse: it seemed to pay homage to the theologians and their regime of truth, but it would restrict their authority once they allow it through their gates.

Galileo had at least one more reason for using the image of the

Two Books. Although he could not prove the truth of Copernicanism, Galileo tried to give the Book of Nature an authority similar to the Book of Scripture. In response to those whose regime of truth rested on God's word as embodied in a Book, Galileo tried to claim that nature was a book too with its own authority. The Book of Nature had to be a sacred book like the Scripture for it to gain authority. So what makes them different then? According to Galileo, the Book of Scripture has an audience while the Book of Nature does not; the former was written with a goal and an addressee in mind, the latter was not. And that's where he would lead himself into contradiction. If nature is a book that was not written to be read, how could Galileo claim that he could read the Book of Nature properly, whereas people like Johannes Kepler and Tycho Brahe presumably could not? Somehow, Galileo needed to read the Book of Nature, but could read it only because it was not meant to be read.

What are we to make of all of this? The good part of the Two Books analogy is that there need not be any conflict, contradiction, or incompatibility between science and religion, or between faith and reason; they actually need each other and complement each other—provided, of course, that we keep our philosophy straight. I am not speaking here in terms of "reconciliation," as if science and religion were just two different ways of expressing single truth. Science masquerading as religion is as unseemly as religion masquerading as science. Instead, they convey two very different kinds of truth. Science has *theories* to help us understand, but they are subject to change—so let us not make science more than what it is. Religion, on the other hand, has *truths* we try to understand, but they never change—so let us not make religion less than what it is.

Attempts to "reconcile" the data of religion with the data of science usually go only one way—"interpreting" the data of religion so as to leave the data of science intact (as if science is always right). Many believe this is what ultimately happened after the "Galileo affair." They consider the case exclusively in terms of either-or. If Galileo was right, the Bible and the Church must have been wrong. Or, if the Bible and the Church were right, Galileo must have been wrong.

The contrary is true. Galileo and his opponents did not understand their clash in terms of religion-versus-science. All parties involved realized that a balance between reason and faith is necessary. Otherwise, the conflict would degenerate into a state in which religious people totally rejected science and its natural laws, and scientists totally rejected the claims of religious truth. All parties were in agreement that we are dealing with *two* different Books here.

This is what we have learned from the "Galileo conflict"— although the core of this understanding is much older. We have become more aware than ever that science reads the *Book of Nature*, whereas the Church reads the *Book of Scripture*. Those two books complement each other, for they have the same Author—they are, in fact, a match made in Heaven. To set them up against each other is a false dichotomy. Cardinal Baronius had already worded it this way at the time, when he said, "The Bible teaches us how to go to heaven, not how the heavens go."

We should keep in mind that Galileo was not condemned by the Church for his astronomy. He was condemned for proclaiming himself an expert in theological matters and for promoting a theory as certain, true, and proven without enough scientific evidence. There was no conflict here between religion and science as such. And that is how it would stay. Like it had done before the Galileo controversy, the Church would continue to cooperate with science, even after Galileo, as if there had never been any "conflict." Catholic cathedrals in Bologna, Florence, Paris, and Rome were constructed to function as solar observatories. No more precise instruments for observing the sun's apparent motion could be found anywhere in the world. When Johannes Kepler posited that planetary orbits were elliptical rather than circular, Catholic astronomer Giovanni Cassini verified Kepler's position through observations he made in the Basilica of San Petronio in the heart of the Papal States. And that is just the least of what the Church did for science.

Church Support for Science

Biblical Support for Science

The French physicist and historian of science Pierre Duhem did groundbreaking work in the history of science when he showed that the doctrines of the Church have been a permanent ally of, rather than an obstacle to, the success of the scientific enterprise in the West. He revealed how it was the metaphysical framework of medieval Catholicism that made modern science possible. In 1215, for instance, the Fourth Lateran Council taught that the universe was created out of nothing at the beginning of time—an idea which would have scandalized both an ancient Greek and a nineteenth-century positivist, but which is now a commonplace of modern cosmology (the astronomer Fr. Georges Lemaître launched in 1929 what is now known as the Big Bang theory).

The Judeo-Christian belief, which holds that nature is not a divine but a created entity, actually opens the way for scientific exploration (otherwise we would not be allowed to "touch" the divine). Because the Judeo-Christian God is a reliable God—not confined inside the Aristotelian box, not capricious like the Olympians in ancient Greece, and not entirely beyond human comprehension like in Islam—the world depends on the laws that God has laid down in creation. Thanks to God's creation, pantheism is stripped of its power and allure. Faith in the one God changes the universe, once inhabited with spirits, deities, and goddesses, into something intelligible, something we can explore. God is the ultimate source of both the order as well as the intelligibility of the universe.

The only way to find out what this order looks like is to "interrogate" the universe by investigation, exploration, and experiment. The door for science has been widely opened. Through scientific experiments we can "read" the thoughts of God, so to speak. This religiously inspired thought has a long history in science. Copernicus's achievements were in fact based on his religious belief that nothing was easier for God than to have the earth move, if he so wished. Kepler's Christian belief told him God would not tolerate the inaccuracy of circular models of planetary movements in astronomy. It is revealing that the "scientific revolution" in the seventeenth century coincided with the period when Christian belief was at its strongest. It was in God that these scientists found reason to investigate nature and trust their own scientific reasoning. The founder of quantum physics, Max Planck, put it well: "It was not by accident that the greatest thinkers of all ages were deeply religious souls." People who come to mind are Johannes Kepler, Isaac Newton, Blaise Pascal, Fr. Gregor Mendel, Louis Pasteur, Fr. George Lemaître, and so many others.

The modern physical sciences were, in fact, made possible by the religious milieu out of which they emerged. It is no accident that modern science first appeared precisely in Christian Europe, where a doctrine of creation held sway. To hold that the world is created is to accept, simultaneously, the two assumptions required for science, namely, that the universe is not divine and that it is marked, through and through, by intelligibility. If the world or nature is considered divine (as it is in many philosophies and mysticisms), then one would never allow oneself to analyze it, dissect it, or perform experiments upon it. But a created world, by definition, is not divine. It is other than God, and in that very otherness, scientists find their freedom to act. At the same time, if the world were unintelligible, no science would get off the ground, since all science is based upon the presumption that nature can be known and understood by the human mind.

It is thus becoming more and more evident, and has been accepted by a growing contingent of historians, that science was born in the cradle of Judeo-Christian Faith, especially during the Late Middle Ages. Here are some of its pioneer crafters: As early as the 7th century, the English Benedictine monk St. Bede studied the sea's tidal currents. At the end of the first millennium, Pope Sylvester II had already used advanced instruments of astronomical observation, in his passion for understanding the order of the universe. He endorsed and promoted study of arithmetic, mathematics, and astronomy, reintroducing to Europe the abacus and armillary sphere, which had been lost to Europe since the end of the Greco-Roman era. He is also said to be the first to introduce in Europe the decimal numeral system using the Arabic numerals.

Very often forgotten is St. Hildegard of Bingen, a Benedictine abbess and Doctor of the Church. She wrote botanical and medicinal texts based on a theological notion ultimately derived from Genesis that all things put on earth are for the use of humans. She was particularly interested in the healing properties of plants, animals, and stones. Then there is St. Albert the Great (also called Albertus

Magnus), the teacher of St. Thomas Aquinas. Albert had quite a track record for his time. He discovered the element arsenic; he experimented with photosensitive chemicals, including silver nitrate; and he made disciplined observations in plant anatomy and animal embryology. During the same time period, Bishop Robert Grosseteste introduced the scientific method, including the concept of falsification, while the Franciscan friar Roger Bacon (1214–1294) established concepts such as hypothesis, experimentation, and verification. In other words, the scientific project, even the scientific method itself, was and is an invention of the Catholic Church.

Hence, what some consider a period of darkness—during the so-called "dark" Middle Ages—was actually the birth of the light of Reason. The great European universities were founded during this prolific era: Bologna, Coimbra, Paris, Oxford, Salamanca, Cambridge, and Padua. Scientists could begin to breathe. Copernicus, Galileo, and Kepler were not at all disturbed by the removal of the earth from the center; rather, they rejoiced in the fact that, with the sun at its center, the whole universe looked more singular than ever. The very structure of the universe was evidence of the Creator's design. Science was invented to give glory to God by examining his laws of nature, not to overthrow God or erase him from existence. The Biblical Book of Wisdom (11:21) says about God, "You have disposed all things by measure, number and weight." And that is what science is about—it is about what can be counted, measured, and quantified. But we must also realize not everything that counts can be counted.

In sum, the creation of the university, the commitment to reason and rational argument, and the overall spirit of inquiry that characterized medieval intellectual life amounted to a gift from the Latin Middle Ages to the modern world. It is a gift that may never be widely acknowledged; perhaps it will always retain the status it has had for the past four centuries as the best-kept secret of Western civilization.

Papal Support for Science

There is a long-standing tradition in the Catholic Church—at least dating as far back as St. Augustine and St. Albert the Great—of advocating the peaceful coexistence of science and religion, and proclaiming that faith and reason can never contradict each other. It is this profoundly Catholic truth that has been affirmed by popes and theologians from the earliest Church to today.

It is no wonder, then, given this tradition, that it was Pope Leo XIII (1878–1903) who could write more than one hundred years ago in his encyclical *Providentissimus Deus* (18):

> no real disagreement can exist between the theologian and the scientist provided each keeps within his own limits. . . . If nevertheless there is a disagreement . . . it should be remembered that the sacred writers, or more truly the Spirit of God who spoke through them, did not wish to teach men such truths [as the inner structure of visible objects] which do not help anyone to salvation; and that, for this reason, rather than trying to provide a scientific exposition of nature, they sometimes describe and treat these matters either in a somewhat figurative language or as the common manner of speech of those times required, and indeed still requires nowadays in everyday life, even amongst most learned people.

Then, just before World War II, Pope Pius XI promoted a renewed dialog between science and religion. Pius XI was also a scholar, and as such he had an openness to science and research like no other pope since Leo XIII. It was this Pontiff who proclaimed St. Albert the Great a Doctor of the Church in 1931. And then in 1936, Pius XI re-established the *Pontifical Academy of Sciences* in order to support serious scientific study within the Catholic Church. In his *Motu Proprio*, the Pontiff said:

> Science, when it is real cognition, is never in contrast with the truth of the Christian faith. Indeed, as is well known to those who study the history of science, it must be recognized that the Roman Pontiffs and the Catholic Church have always fostered the research of the learned in the experimental field.

It was at his dear Academy that Pope Pius XI gave his last pontifical address before he died in 1939; not surprisingly, it was on the harmonious relation between science and religion. In it, he quoted from the *Book of Wisdom*, "you have disposed all things by measure and number and weight" (11:20), and then the Holy Father continued:

It is like going into an immense laboratory of chemistry, of physics, of astronomy. Few indeed can admire the profound beauty of such words as well as those who make sciences their profession. . . . The created world receives weight, number, and measure through the hands of God. This is true for everything: for the greatest as much as for the smallest.

His successor, Pope Pius XII, carried on this Catholic approach to the sciences. During his address to the *Pontifical Academy of Sciences*, on November 22, 1951, the Pontiff declared unreservedly that "true science discovers God in an ever-increasing degree—as though God were waiting behind every door opened by science." Indeed, in the words of G.K. Chesterton, science is racing toward the mysteries of faith with the speed of an express train.

Pope John Paul's Encyclical *Fides et Ratio* (Faith and Reason) revived the image of the "Book of Nature" that Galileo had used:

in reasoning about nature, the human being can rise to God: "From the greatness and beauty of created things comes a corresponding perception of their Creator" (Wis. 13:5). This is to recognize as a first stage of divine Revelation the marvelous "book of nature", which, when read with the proper tools of human reason, can lead to knowledge of the Creator. If human beings with their intelligence fail to recognize God as Creator of all, it is not because they lack the means to do so, but because their free will and their sinfulness place an impediment in the way.

And during an address to the Pontifical Academy of Sciences, given on October 31, 2008, his successor, Pope Benedict XVI, reinforced the same message:

The imagery of nature as a book has its roots in Christianity and has been held dear by many scientists. Galileo saw nature as a book whose author is God in the same way that Scripture has God as its author. It is a book whose history, whose evolution, whose "writing" and meaning, we "read" according to the different approaches of the sciences, while all the time presupposing the foundational presence of the author who has wished to reveal himself therein. This image also helps us to understand that the world, far from originating out of chaos, resembles an ordered book; it is a cosmos. Notwithstanding elements of the irrational, chaotic and the destructive in the long processes of change in the cosmos, matter as such is "legible". It has an inbuilt "mathematics".

In 2013, Pope Francis would take a similar stand in his Apostolic Exhortation *Evangelii Gaudium* (#243):

The Church has no wish to hold back the marvelous progress of science. On the contrary, she rejoices and even delights in acknowledging the enormous potential that God has given to the human mind. Whenever the sciences—rigorously focused on their specific field of inquiry—arrive at a conclusion which reason cannot refute, faith does not contradict it.

Today the Church continues its involvement in scientific pursuits through the Pontifical Academy of Sciences. In doing so, the Church has also reflected further on the Galileo case. In a 1939 address to the Pontifical Academy of Sciences, Pope Pius XII had called Galileo one of the "most audacious heroes of research . . . not afraid of the stumbling blocks and the risks on the way." And in 1983, Pope John Paul II held a conference celebrating the 350th anniversary of the publication of Galileo's *Dialogue Concerning the Two Chief World Systems*, at which he remarked that the experience of the Galileo case had led the Church "to a more mature attitude and a more accurate grasp of the authority proper to her," enabling her better to distinguish between "essentials of the faith" and the "scientific systems of a given age." The Pontiff called Galileo's clash with the Church a "tragic mutual incomprehension" in which both sides were at fault. Although both were at fault, they also both learned from this experience.

All of this testifies that the Catholic Church has no fear of science or scientific discovery, in spite of the fabricated myth of a clash between the two. The Church stands in a long tradition of defending the position that faith and reason—or religion and science, for that matter—do not contradict each other but rather complement each other, as coming from the same source, God. Standing within this strong and solid tradition, Vatican II declared very concisely and plainly in *Gaudium et Spes* (36) that

if methodical investigation within every branch of learning is carried out in a genuinely scientific manner and in accord with moral norms, it never truly conflicts with faith, for earthly matters and the concerns of faith derive from the same God.

This view is well put and summarized in the Catechism of the Catholic Church (CCC 159):

> The humble and persevering investigator of the secrets of nature is being led, as it were, by the hand of God in spite of himself, for it is God, the conserver of all things, who made them what they are.

Myth 5
The Holocaust, a Catholic Plot

Although there is no way to be sufficiently sensitive to the incomprehensible suffering the Holocaust caused, we cannot examine the role Catholicism played in this drama without going into more details about the Holocaust.

There are at least two myths about the relationship between the Catholic Church and the Holocaust that need to be addressed. One is that the Catholic Church actually supported the Holocaust, and that Nazism itself was rooted in Catholicism. The other is that the Catholic Church, more in particular Pope Pius XII, did nothing to prevent or at least stop the Holocaust.

The Driving Force behind the Holocaust

Rooting out Christianity

Nazism is often perceived as being an offshoot of Catholic anti-Semitism. Nothing is further from the truth. On a closer look, Nazism turns out to be a fervently anti-Catholic ideology occasionally concealed behind a Catholic face.

Christianity certainly looms in the personal histories of the Nazis. Adolf Hitler was born Catholic (although he had never practiced the Catholic faith since childhood), Joseph Goebbels went to a Franciscan boarding school, Reinhard Heydrich was Catholic, and so was Heinrich Müller. Hermann Goering, on the other hand, had a mixed Catholic-Protestant parentage, while Rudolf Hess, Martin Bormann, Albert Speer, and Adolf Eichmann were from Protestant backgrounds. But even if many in the Nazi leadership were Catholics, the most we can say is that they were *former* Catholics who had renounced their religion and had converted to neo-paganism, as I will show shortly.

A special case was Heinrich Himmler, a devoted Catholic as a student. He made it his business to assemble an extensive library about the Jesuit Order. He even dreamt at one stage of training his elite *Waffen SS* combat troops along Jesuit lines and went so far as to propose the principal officers undergo a form of Ignatius's *Spiritual Exercises*—adapted, however, to a mad blend of the new Nordic cult of Wodin, Siegfried, the Holy Grail, and the Teutonic Knights of old. The plan never succeeded, but even Hitler knew of it and joked about Himmler as "our very own Ignatius Loyola." So there may be some Catholic roots here, but they were largely overgrown by plants from very different origins.

The prevailing myth spread by the media is that Nazism had Catholic roots and was actually the result of Catholic anti-Semitism. Fans of this myth would also point out that not only were former Catholics well presented in the Nazi leadership, but so were many Catholics in the German population who welcomed the rise of Nazism in 1933. If that perception is true, we should find out what their reasons could have been for supporting Nazism. Probably, one of them was that they were persuaded by the statement on "positive Christianity" in Article 24 of the 1920 Nazi Party Platform, which read:

> We demand the freedom of all religious confessions in the state, insofar as they do not jeopardize the state's existence or conflict with the manners and moral sentiments of the Germanic race. The Party as such upholds the point of view of a positive Christianity without tying itself confessionally to any one confession. It combats the Jewish-materialistic spirit at home and abroad and is convinced that a permanent recovery of our people can only be achieved from within on the basis of the common good before individual good.

Despite the open anti-Semitism of this statement and its linkage between confessional "freedom" and a nationalistic, racialized understanding of morality, many Christians in Germany at the time misread this as an affirmation of Christian values.

Obviously, many average Catholics, like most other Germans, were not fully aware of the dangers of National Socialism. Some saw the Nazis as a potential ally against the spread of Communism.

Bishop Christian Schreiber of Berlin, for example, granted permission for Catholics to join the party for this reason. Many German bishops and priests, however, were alarmed by the Nazis and their anti-Semitic speeches, radical nationalistic tone, and their clear willingness to use violence and intimidation. In early 1931, the bishops conference of the Cologne region condemned National Socialism, followed by the bishops of the region of Paderborn and Freiburg. The Catholic press and the Catholic German Center Party were also distinctly hostile to the Nazis.

Initially, Hitler and the Nazis tried to present a moderate and reassuring face to Catholics. But the instinctive reaction of many Catholics to the Nazis was a negative one, and only small numbers of Catholics voted for the National Socialists in the elections prior to 1933. It was soon after the elections that the Nazi Party began to show its true face. Hermann Göring banned all Catholic newspapers in Cologne on the claim that Catholics were illegally engaging in politics. The ban was lifted soon after, but Catholics had gotten the message. A short time later, thugs from the *Sturmabteilung* (SA), the so-called Brownshirts, stormed a gathering of the Christian trade unions and the Catholic Center Party, and brutalized many of those in attendance.

Catholics next witnessed the attacks on the Catholic press. A special "Editors' Law" was decreed in December 1933 with the intention of curbing all speech by requiring that all editors join the Literary Chamber of the Third Reich. The Chamber, part of Josef Goebbels's Propaganda Ministry, decided what could be published and what not. The law essentially ended the Catholic press in Germany. Catholic newspapers and publications soon closed their doors as they were unable to comply with government limitations on freedom and unwilling to print Nazi propaganda on such horrendous issues as enforced sterilization and euthanasia. At the start of 1933, there were over 400 daily Catholic newspapers in Germany. By 1935, there were none left.

The next step was that German Catholics were discouraged from sending their children to Catholic schools. Nazi propaganda called those schools disloyal and havens of corruption, and families were eventually required to appear before authorities to declare officially why they had decided to betray the regime. More anti-Catholic measurements soon followed, although still very cautiously introduced.

Gradually things became undeniably clear. On June 6, 1941, Martin Bormann, head of the Nazi Party Chancellery, private secretary to Adolf Hitler and one of the most powerful figures in the Third Reich, issued a secret decree for all *Gauleiters* (regional party leaders) of the Reich regarding the true intentions of the Nazi regime toward the Christian churches:

> More and more the people must be separated from the churches and their organs the pastors. . . . Just as the deleterious influences of astrologers, seers and other fakers are eliminated and suppressed by the State, so must the possibility of church influence also be totally removed. . . . Not until this has happened, does the state leadership have influence on the individual citizens. Not until then are the people and Reich secure in their existence for all time.

The Catholic Church responded directly to these developments. Albert Einstein (who was Jewish), reacting to the Nazi persecution of the Jews, praised the Catholic Church but was dismayed at the lack of outcry or assistance from secular establishments. He said:

> Only the Catholic Church protested against the Hitlerian onslaught on liberty. Up till then I had not been interested in the Church, but today I feel a great admiration for the Church, which alone has had the courage to struggle for spiritual truth and moral liberty.

In 1943, *Time* magazine praised the papacy for taking a powerful stand against totalitarianism:

> The Catholic Church . . . insists on the dignity of the individual whom God created in his own image and for a decade has vigorously protested against the cruel persecution of the Jews as a violation of God's tabernacle.

From the beginning, Catholic leaders were more suspicious of National Socialism than all other established forces in Germany—media, academia, business, or the arts. They were even more apprehensive than their Protestant counterparts. Nationalism was not as deeply embedded in the German Catholic Church, so the rabid anti-Catholicism of men such as Alfred Rosenberg, a leading Nazi ideologue during the Nazi rise to power, raised early concerns among Catholic leaders in Germany and at the Vatican. In 1934, the Vatican put Rosenberg's book on the index of forbidden books for scorning and rejecting "all dogmas of the Catholic Church, indeed the very fundamentals of the Christian religion."

It became more and more obvious that the long-term aim of the Nazis was to de-Christianize Germany. Hitler believed that in the long run National Socialism and religion would not be able to co-exist, and stressed repeatedly that Nazism was a secular ideology, founded on modern "science"—the pseudo-science of racial superiority, that is. Nazi ideology required the subordination of the Church to the State and could not accept an autonomous establishment whose legitimacy did not spring from the government. As a consequence, from the very beginning, the Catholic Church faced general persecution, suppression, and oppression. Aggressive anti-Church radicals such as Joseph Goebbels and Martin Bormann saw the conflict with the Church as a primary concern, and anti-church and anti-clerical sentiments were strong among grassroots party activists. To many Nazis, Catholics were suspected of insufficient patriotism, or even of disloyalty to the Fatherland, and of serving the interests of "sinister alien forces."

Adolf Hitler did have some regard for the organizational power of Catholicism, but towards its teachings he showed only the sharpest hostility. To Hitler, Christianity was a religion fit only for slaves, and he detested its ethics. Based on political considerations, Hitler was prepared to restrain his anti-clericalism, seeing danger in strengthening the Church by persecution; but he certainly intended a showdown after the war. Joseph Goebbels, who led the Nazi persecution of the Catholic clergy, wrote that there was "an insoluble opposition between the Christian and a heroic-German world view." Hitler's chosen deputy, Martin Bormann, saw Christianity and Nazism as "incompatible," as did the official Nazi philosopher, Alfred Rosenberg, who wrote as early as 1930 that Catholics were among the chief enemies of the Germans.

As a consequence, the Nazis claimed jurisdiction over all collective and social activity, interfering with Catholic schooling, youth groups, workers' clubs, and cultural societies. Hitler moved quickly to eliminate political Catholicism, rounding up members of the Catholic aligned Bavarian People's Party and the Catholic Center Party, which ceased to exist in early July of 1933. Meanwhile, Vice Chancellor Franz von Papen, on Hitler's request, negotiated a Reich concordat with the Holy See, which prohibited clergy from participating in politics. Hitler then proceeded to close all Catholic institutions whose functions were not strictly religious.

As to the question of whether Nazism had Catholic roots, we must come to the conclusion that there were no such roots. Quite the opposite, Nazism wanted to root out all traces of Catholicism. The Dachau concentration camp, for instance, was used by the Nazis for many of its most hated enemies—among them Catholic priests. Indeed, of the 2,720 clergy sent to Dachau, 2,579 were Catholic priests; most of them were Polish priests, 1,748 in all; of the 1,034 priests who died in the camp, 868 were also Polish. The priests were housed in a special "priest block" and were targeted for especially brutal treatment by the SS guards.

It is estimated that at least 3,000 more Polish priests were sent to other concentration camps, including Auschwitz, while priests from all across Europe were condemned to death and labor camps. Records show that 300 priests died at Sachsenhausen, 780 at Mauthausen, and 5,000 at Buchenwald. These numbers do not include the priests who were murdered en route to the camps or who died from diseases and exhaustion in the inhuman cattle cars used to transport victims. Several thousand nuns were also sent to camps or killed on the way.

Who could still claim that Catholicism, or Christianity in general, was an ally of Nazism? They were definitely not allies, but radical foes. Their principles and goals could not be more dramatically opposed to one another.

Satanic Motivations

When seeing the actions of people like Hitler, almost everyone knows that we are dealing here with *evil*. The question is, though, what is the origin of such evil? I think most people would find it hard to believe that one man, Adolf Hitler, could have caused the evil of the Holocaust and the other evils of the Nazi Party, on his own and by his own power. There must be more to the story.

When studying what lies behind the Holocaust, we come across an intricate network of ideological and spiritual forces. Schoeman has an excellent overview of this issue, from which I heavily borrowed for this discussion.

First of all, there was a quasi-scientific preparation for the Holocaust. The anti-Semitism of the Nazi regime did not stem from anything like Catholic anti-Semitism; instead it was based on the ideology of eugenics—a version of Darwinism, originally developed by Francis Galton, which advocates the improvement of human genetic traits through the promotion of higher reproduction of people with desired traits (positive eugenics), and reduced reproduction of people with less-desired or undesired traits (negative eugenics). The main part of that campaign was to improve the human race and create a nation of "supermen" through selective breeding. The Nazi persecution of the Jews had as its sole aim the eradication of the Jewish race as a race, the freeing of the world from the "taint" of Jewish blood.

In Schoeman's wording: "The issue was not the religion of Judaism; it was the racial identity of the Jews. . . . Being baptized was not an escape; in fact, being born and raised Christian, by parents who had already converted to Christianity, did not make the slightest difference to being marked for extermination. . . . It was applied Darwinism, not applied Christianity" (pp. 181–2). In other words, it was a massive eugenics program, not based on principles of "Christianity" but on principles of "Social Darwinism."

Second, there was an intellectual preparation for the Holocaust. The beliefs of intrinsic superiority of the "Aryan race" and the inferiority of the Jews can be traced back to the Second Reich. Bismarck's "blood and iron" policies had created a powerful, even dominant nation, ready for a strident economic and political nationalism. The myth of a "master race" destined to conquer the world and subdue "lesser races" gripped many Germans. The philosophical foundations of this idea had already been laid by Arthur de Gobineau and Houston Chamberlain.

Third, there was a spiritual preparation for the Holocaust. From the outset, the pseudo-science of racial superiority was deeply intertwined with occultism. There were many links in this chain. One of them was Madame Blavatsky with her version of occultism known as Theosophy. She claimed to have received her occult doctrines during seven years she spent in Tibet studying under Hindu masters. Her contempt for Jews and Judaism was undisguised. The swastika figured prominently in the seal of her society and was finally adopted as a dominant symbol by Hitler.

Another link in the connection with occultism is Guido List who blended Theosophy with the occult use of the old Germanic runes and other occult practices, worshipping the Norse god Wotan. Early in his adult life, Hitler was a follower of List and probably even a formal member of his occult society. A third link in the connection is the Thule Society. Thule was a mythological Northern land from which the Aryans supposedly had come, apparently identified with Atlantis. The Society's principal aims were the monitoring of Jews and their activities and the distribution of anti-Semitic material. The group bought an obscure Munich weekly and turned it into the official paper of the Nazi party. Many of those who set the direction of the Third Reich came from the Thule Society—people such as Alfred Rosenberg and Rudolf Hess.

Another important link was Dietrich Eckart from the Thule Society. He predicted the imminent coming of a German messiah who would free Germany from the chains of Christianity. He also claimed to have "initiated" Hitler into occultism—a rite by which "higher centers" are opened, enabling extrasensory powers. In reality, it entails the introduction of demonic entities into the individual. On at least one occasion, Hitler referred to Eckart as his "John the Baptizer."

Then there was Alfred Rosenberg who eventually became the official ideologist of the Nazi party and the primary "theologian" of its new religion. He was very explicit about the rejection of Christianity in favor of Nazism's own new Germanic, nationalist pagan religion. As he wrote: "We now realize that the central supreme values of the Roman and the Protestant Churches, being a negative Christianity, do not respond to our soul." He drew up the program for the

"National Reich Church," which cleared away from its altars all cru-cifixes, Bibles, and pictures of saints; on the altars there must be nothing but *Mein Kampf*, he said, and to the left of the altar a sword.

Finally, there is Heinrich Himmler, who was never without his copy of the Hindu scriptures. He deeply believed in Eastern ideas such as reincarnation and karma. He established an institute in Ber-lin to study the potential of harnessing occult forces of power for the war effort, including black magic, spiritualist mediums, pendu-lum practitioners, and astrologers.

Is any more evidence needed that Nazism was not rooted in Christianity? It was a revival of a romanticized Teutonic paganism, replete with the revival of ancient gods, rites, rituals, and symbols, and imbued with an active occultism coming from Eastern religions via Theosophy.

In retrospect, all of the above looks like a master plan. Who or what could have orchestrated such a "masterpiece," with all pieces falling into place? I see only one possible answer: this master plan is beyond mere human power. Behind all of this, there is a much wider, deeper, and stronger warfare going on between the "economy of salvation" and the "economy of perdition." St. Ignatius of Loyola would speak of a cosmic warfare between Good and Evil, between God and Lucifer (not as two eternal principles locked in permanent conflict, for Satan and other demons are fallen Angels made by God as good Angels). Two cosmic powers—intelligent good and intelli-gent evil, personified in God and Lucifer—are locked in a life-and-death struggle for the allegiance of all human beings. While alive in this world, no one can escape the constant attentions of both God and Lucifer.

The "economy of salvation" is led by God who wants as many people as possible to be saved, so they can end up enjoying eternal life in beatitude with God. The "economy of perdition" is led by an intelligent agent who strives to lead as many souls as possible to damnation. This latter agent was, in the words of Schoeman, "given the name 'Satan' in the Old Testament, which is simply the Hebrew for 'adversary,' since he is the adversary of man's salvation" (p. 196).

Only the religious "eye" is able to see all of history as a cosmic and constant warfare between God and Satan, waged everywhere and daily. It "sees" how the power of evil and the darkness of Satan enabled a man like Hitler to spellbind and enslave the minds and spirits of millions, creating hell ahead of time, right here on earth. This explains how such people had sold their souls by following "orders" that stem from sources far beyond their own resources. Only religious people are able to see this dimension in a history that historians usually miss. As a matter of fact, the reality of evil goes far beyond material and physical powers; it goes even far beyond what human beings can do on their own. After all, could Hitler have ever done what he did by relying on human power alone? Satan was and is happy to lend such people some "spiritual" help from "beyond," giving them more than mere human power—extraordinary, super-human power.

The core of the story is that Hitler—and those with him—had made a pact with the devil. There are many indications that Hitler's relationship to the satanic was intentional, explicit, and extensive. Schoeman mentions no less an authority than the current chief exorcist of Rome, Father Gabriele Amorth, who stated explicitly that the senior officials of the Nazi Party were actively involved with Satanism and that "certainly Hitler was consecrated to Satan" (p. 232). Later on, Pope Benedict XVI would write in his *Memoirs* that "Hitler was a demonic figure." Let us not forget that Dietrich Eckart from the Thule Society had "initiated" Hitler into occultism. Strikingly, Schoeman uses the image of a busy two-way traffic: "in one direction, the Nazis feeding the forces of hell with their cruelty, their murder, their occult rites, worship and practices, their idolatry; in the other direction, hell feeding them with power, inspiration, lust, and success in their malevolent undertakings" (p. 198). As Schoeman further argues:

> One cannot read very much about the Holocaust without being struck, over and over again, by the indications of diabolical inspiration for what happened. It appears in the extraordinary cruelty of the Nazis, in the philosophy of their leaders, in their explicit hatred of God and religion, in their determination to wipe out Christianity as well as Judaism, in their open embrace of paganism and occultism, in their sexual perversity, and in their satanic, cultic practices. (p. 245)

God's Chosen People

The main target of Nazism was the Jews, God's chosen people. What does it mean to be "God's Chosen People"? A cursory reading of the Old Testament is enough to tell us what this "secret" of Judaism entails.

First, there is God's long and meticulous preparation of this people to become "a light for the nations" (Is. 42:6; 49:6; 60:3), and to ultimately become ready to be the cradle where the Messiah could be born. God began his history of the Jews with Abraham and promised him that "by you all the families of the earth shall be blessed" (Gen. 12:3). Then he further refined Israel through his prophets so they would be fit enough to bring blessing—and eventually the ultimate blessing of the Redeemer—to all of humanity. God chose Abraham and those born from him to be the covenanted community that God needs for Judaism to do its work in the world.

Second, this preparation also entailed that Israel had to be purified from the influence of "false gods." If God was to be on a uniquely intimate basis with the Jews and eventually to become one of them (the Incarnation), then they would have to be free from all involvement with other deities, free from all spiritual pollution. Unlike we often think nowadays, those "other deities" are not merely carved images of false superstition and human imagination but they are real—real gods, fallen angels, demons, or devils. As Schoeman points out,

> The 'gods' that the pagans worshipped truly existed and truly fulfilled the role of gods to their adherents—that is, in return for adoration, reference, and sacrifice they returned services to their adherents. . . . The unique revelation of Judaism was that in addition to these 'gods,' there is only one true God, a different sort of god, absolutely unique and absolutely sovereign, Himself uncreated, who created all the other gods as well as everything else that exists. As the Psalm (95:3) says, "For the Lord is God, the mighty God, the great King over all the gods." (pp. 46–47)

Third, as a consequence of this unique relationship with God, the Jews had to be separated from the Gentiles, from those who sacrifice to their own gods, the demons. This separation of the Jews was imposed on them by God so they could fulfill the mission for which they had been chosen. The Jews had to go on as a separate and distinct people, remaining true to the worship of the one true God, remaining free from spiritual pollution coming from the worship of other gods. For Schoeman,

> This exclusionary aspect of Judaism was required for the Jews to be able to fulfill the role for which they had been chosen—that of bringing the Messiah, God born as man, into the world. . . . They were able to maintain this necessary distinctness for the two thousand years between Abraham and Jesus. . . . The survival of the Jews as a distinct people for another two thousand years, without a land and under continual persecution, is no less miraculous. (p. 66)

It should not surprise us then that God's adversary, Satan, does not like "God's Chosen People." The primary motivation behind the Holocaust was sheer, raw hatred of the Jews, of those who are called God's "Chosen People." Given God's special love for the Jews—as described in all books of the Bible—it is logical that God's enemy, who is the diabolic mastermind behind the Holocaust, is particularly interested in *them*, for they have been called to bring blessing—and eventually the ultimate blessing of the Redeemer—to all of humanity. The "economy of perdition" is completely hostile to this "economy of salvation."

In the Holocaust, according to Schoeman, this hatred against the Jews was expressed in three ways—trying to eliminate Jews and Judaism, causing the Jews as much suffering, pain, anguish, and humiliation as humanly possible, and finally, by trying to damn as many Jews as possible (pp. 248–49). As a consequence, in Schoeman's words,

> the concentration camps were not only designed to torture and kill the Jews, but they were also designed to dehumanize them, to wear down their moral resistance, and to cause them to act in ways that would offend God—either by rebelling against Him or by committing suicide (which was a frequent occurrence at Auschwitz, primarily by throwing oneself against the electrified

fence). . . . For the adversary wished not only to see the Jews suffer and die, but worse, to be damned. (pp. 248–49)

The adversary's special hatred against the Jews is further inflamed by the fact that Christ himself was a Jew. Cardinal Jean-Marie Lustiger—who was born and raised Jewish, converted to Catholicism, and became Archbishop of Paris from 1981 until his resignation in 2005—has pointed out that the fundamental root of anti-Semitism on a spiritual level is hatred of Christ. He wrote:

Hitler's anti-Semitism had its roots in the anti-Semitism of the Enlightenment and not in Christian anti-Semitism. . . . The Jews, the Jewish people, exist because God has chosen them. They have no other reason for existing, not even national sentiment. . . . The existence of the chosen people concerns God's plan for humanity: if Israel exists, it is because God has chosen this people for the purpose of saving all mankind.

Cardinal Lustiger is also very definite about the diabolical roots and goals of the Nazis:

These men are only weak creatures, puppets, immersed in an absolute evil that surpasses them. . . . Those men we see are only the servile actors. . . . When as a child I spent time in Nazi Germany, I had understood: Nazism's aim was more than Promethean, it was Satanic. . . . This utterly overwhelming conflict can be understood only within the mystery of the suffering Messiah and the redemption with the struggle it implies.

Is there any reason left to call Nazism a movement inspired by Catholic principles and elements? To think there is surely requires a complete denial of the facts.

Did Hitler Succeed?

Hitler certainly succeeded in the short run. Not only was he successful in directly killing more than six million Jews in his gas chambers, but he also indirectly dehumanized them by wearing down the moral resistance of those who ended up cursing God or committing suicide—either to avoid deportation or, once in the camps, by throwing themselves against the electrified fence.

But even in the long term, Hitler succeeded more than he could have ever wished for. After the Holocaust, many Jews felt that their being chosen by God was the cause of near extinction by the Nazis. As the Jewish theologian David Novak puts it,

> There are Jews today who ... have concluded that if the affirmation of chosenness by God is the cause of near extinction, Jews must root that affirmation out entirely. And for some Jews, this denial of election ... lives at a primal, emotional level: "Since God's choice of us Jews has led to death and destruction, we now unchoose Him!". . . They've chosen to be unchosen.

As a consequence, those Jews no longer wanted to keep their part of the Covenant, for they felt abandoned by God as a people.

Those who did so actually enforced what Hitler could not have done better—separating themselves from God. They had lost the reason as to why they had been chosen—the reason being to be the people that God needs to be His witness in this world. They decided to be no longer trustees of God's covenant with the world; they no longer could understand the divine purpose for which God had chosen them; they no longer would know for whom they have survived the suffering of the Holocaust—which is actually a very sad outcome. Novak again:

> We were chosen to be the trustees of God's Torah, and this is why we must survive as a people, even if it entails walking a dangerous path in this world ... the Jews' chosenness is best lived for "and died for" when we understand the uniquely divine purpose for which God chose us.

Sadly enough, once the Jews have forgotten being chosen or rejected it, they have lost their reason for existing.

This outcome has currently affected a large part of Judaism. If the tragedy of the Holocaust has alienated the Jews from their trust in and worship of God, that might be a tragedy as great as the deaths themselves. It did permeate and destroy Judaism to a large extent and gave Hitler the posthumous victory no Jew would want to give him. And yet it happened, for Satan keeps working.

Three important pillars of the Jewish faith are the following according to Schoeman (pp. 136ff): (1) God is all-good and faithful;

(2) he has a special love for his chosen people; and (3) he has the power to affect human destiny. All these Jewish pillars were shaken in the aftermath of the Holocaust. Elie Wiesel, for instance, a Romanian-born Jewish American, would exclaim, "I believe during the Holocaust the covenant was broken." Rabbi Arthur Herzberg was another Jew who expressed his loss of faith this way: "I could not return to the Orthodox faith in God. I would not forgive Him for the Holocaust, and I would not absolve Him by agreeing that the death camps had existed in a realm that he could not control." And Rabbi Richard Rubenstein would exclaim "We are alone in a silent, unfeeling cosmos . . . for omnipotent Nothingness is Lord of All Creation."

Elie Wiesel is probably one of the most audible Jewish voices in this attack on God. He claims to have been the first to use the word *Holocaust*, alluding to Abraham's sacrifice of Isaac. He claims also that the Jewish survivors of the death camps had every reason in the world to become ferocious nihilists, anarchists, carriers of fear and nightmare. His words are prophetic. He declares himself the accuser, and God the accused.

Schoeman rightly remarks, "There is a tragic irony in this, for the heart of being a Jew is fidelity to God and faith in his goodness" (p.145). Of course, not all Jews lost their faith in the God of Abraham, Isaac, and Jacob because of the Holocaust. Schoeman quotes a Jewish Holocaust theologian: "Jews who observed the rites and rituals of their tradition were 'able to face life with dignity, and death with serenity.'" Many even went to their deaths with a profession of faith on their lips, says another. A beautiful example of Jewish faith is provided in the autobiography of Mel Mermelstein, a seventeen-year-old Jew who was deported to Auschwitz, but survived:

> My uncle placed his hand upon my head and said: ". . . He does not forget. Sometimes it seems as if He needs time to assimilate everything He has seen, and to react to it and give recompense. But you'll see it, Moishele, you're young enough. You'll see. He does not forget!"

Nevertheless, we must agree with Schoeman:

> The Holocaust presents a horribly difficult trial for Jewish theology. When Christians are faced with great persecution and suffer-

ing, they are theologically better equipped to deal with them, since Jesus Himself was faced with the same apparent contradiction between God's goodness and sovereignty and the exorbitant demands of suffering placed upon his faithful servants. (p. 150)

Indeed, for Jews this may be a harder challenge. This is also one of the reasons why Wiesel and some other Jews have shied away from using the term *Holocaust*—the Hebrew word "ola" means "burnt offering." Instead they prefer to speak of *Shoah* as used in Isaiah 47:11. They like this word better because connecting Hitler's mass murder with the Biblical expression for "sacrifice" would, so they believe, exonerate all those involved from their responsibility. But is it really a better choice? Schoeman argues convincingly that it is not (p. 177). The text of Isaiah 47:11 says, "But evil shall come upon you, for which you cannot atone; disaster [shoah] shall fall upon you, which you will not be able to expiate." This is said to the infamous "whore of Babylon." So, Schoeman continues, "The reason there is no atonement in the 'shoah' that overtakes her is not that suffering cannot atone for sin, but rather that the culprit here is beyond redemption!" Denying the aspect of human sacrifice is exactly the reason why Judaism could not accept Jesus of Nazareth as the Messiah, given that he ended up as that sort of a "human sacrifice." The entire theology of Christianity revolves around the role of sacrifice. And the Holocaust too may only be understandable in terms of sacrifice. Later on, the Hindu Mohandas Gandhi would call "worship without sacrifice" an absurdity of the modern age.

The Christian response to Elie Wiesel's angst was well presented by the Catholic writer François Mauriac who wrote a foreword to Wiesel's autobiographical *Night*. Wiesel recounts witnessing the hanging of a young child in the camp, and Mauriac muses:

What did I say to him? Did I speak of that other Jew, his brother, who may have resembled him—the Crucified, whose Cross has conquered the world? Did I affirm that the stumbling block to his faith was the cornerstone of mine, and that the conformity between the Cross and the suffering of men was in my eyes the key to that impenetrable mystery whereon the faith of his childhood had perished? ... If the Eternal is the Eternal, the last word for each one of us belongs to Him. This is what I should have told this Jewish child. But I could only embrace him, weeping.

Another Catholic response to Elie Wiesel was given by a Jewish theologian, St. Edith Stein, who became Catholic and a Carmelite nun before the beginning of World War II. From the beginning of the Nazi takeover of Germany in 1993, she saw what was happening to the Jews in the light of the Cross:

> I spoke with the Savior to tell him that I realized it was his Cross that was now being laid upon the Jewish people, that the few who understood this had the responsibility of carrying it in the name of all, and that I myself was willing to do this, if he would only show me how.

St. Edith Stein was soon shown the way. As she and her sister Rosa were led from their convent in Holland by the SS guards to be taken to Auschwitz, she said to her sister "Come, let us go for our people." When Pope Benedict XVI visited Auschwitz in 2006, he asked the question "Where was God in those days?" And he answered,

> We cannot peer into God's mysterious plan—we see only piece-meal . . . when all is said and done, we must continue to cry out humbly yet insistently to God: Rouse yourself! Do not forget mankind, your creature!

Did the Catholic Church Protest?

Local Responses

On January 30, 1933, Adolf Hitler was officially appointed chancellor by the aged President Paul von Hindenburg. A mere month later, on February 27, the infamous Reichstag Fire (a plot concocted by the Nazis) gave Hitler the pretext to establish a dictatorship through the so-called Enabling Act that was passed in March of 1933. The act bestowed sweeping powers on the government, including setting aside key elements of basic rights, for four years. In the lead-up to the 1933 Nazi coup, several German Catholic leaders had been rather outspoken in their criticism of Nazism. However, following the Nazi takeover, the Catholic Church sought an accord with the Government. After Hitler signed a concordat with the Vatican on

July 20, 1933—which seemed to guarantee the freedoms of the Catholic Church and the continuance of parochial schooling—the bishops revoked their condemnation and told their flocks to obey the new civil authority.

It took a while for the Church in Germany to realize what was really happening in Germany after Hitler's coup. Early in 1931, the bishops conference of the Cologne region condemned National Socialism, followed by the bishops of the region of Paderborn and Freiburg. The Catholic press and the Catholic German Center Party were also distinctly hostile to the Nazis. For their part, Hitler and the Nazis tried to present a moderate and reassuring face to Catholics. But the instinctive reaction of most Catholics to the Nazis was a negative one, and only small numbers of Catholics voted for the National Socialists in the elections prior to 1933. Yet, these were very confusing times for the Catholic Church in Germany.

A good example of how confusing these times were is Cardinal Michael von Faulhaber of Munich. He had been a member of a group called "Friends of Israel" and had a menorah emblazoned on his bishop's coat of arms. In 1933, he responded to the new political developments with three Advent sermons, entitled "Judaism, Christianity, and Germany." In these sermons, more theological than political, he affirmed the Jewish origins of the Christian religion, the continuity of the Old and New Testaments of the Bible, and the importance of the Christian tradition to Germany. This magnificent trio of Advent sermons caused such anger among the Nazis that the sale of the published edition of his sermons was banned by the government.

Unfortunately, the Cardinal was not always as outspoken in his statements against the Nazis, at least not in the beginning. He had always been reluctant to give his full allegiance to the preceding Weimar Republic which he called "the godless Republic." He joined the other German bishops in telling the faithful to give Hitler's new regime a chance in the vain hope that the chancellor would uphold the terms of the new Concordat with the Vatican. But soon the Nazis would shut down the theology department of the University of Munich because Cardinal Faulhaber had refused to accept faculty who supported Hitler. It took much courage to oppose orders from such a brutal regime.

In the midst of all of this, we have to realize that these were very confusing times, particularly for the Church leaders right in the middle of it. Take for instance the Bishop of Trier, Franz Rudolf Bornewasser. In 1933, he had declared, "with raised heads and firm step we have entered the new Reich." But gradually his eyes were opened. When the 1935 German *Farmer's Almanac* had replaced every single Christian feast day with a pagan celebration, the Bishop voiced his protest as follows:

> I am surprised and deeply shocked that the Reich Agricultural Corporation, to which every German farmer, man and woman, must belong, should have offered this Almanac . . . it is a deep insult to every Christian and Catholic feeling.

A few years later, in 1937, it was the same bishop of Trier who complained of the Nazi's intent to eliminate the celebration of Christmas. In his New Year's Eve sermon at the close of the year, he said:

> This artificially stirred-up old Germanic pagan Consecration of Fire is meant as a direct challenge to the highest mystery of our religion, the Incarnation of Jesus Christ on the Holy Night of Bethlehem. . . . Christian Fathers and Mothers! Now you know the real meaning of the celebration of the Winter Solstice. Up to now it had been concealed behind a mask, but today that mask has been dropped.

In August 1935, the bishops of Germany had already presented at Fulda a pastoral letter warning of the Nazi "campaign of annihilation against Christianity." By 1937, the church hierarchy in Germany, which had initially attempted to cooperate with the new government, had become highly disillusioned. More and more Church leaders began to raise their voices in public, after seeing more clearly the true nature of Nazism. Although the earliest concerns were more of an ecclesiastical rather than humanitarian nature, they would gradually widen in scope and go beyond specific Catholic issues and concerns.

One of the most firm and consistent bishops to oppose the Nazis was Cardinal Konrad Graf von Preysing. In 1935, he was appointed as Bishop of Berlin—the capital of Nazi Germany. Preysing was loathed by Hitler, who said "the foulest of carrion are those who come clothed in the cloak of humility and the foulest of these is Count Preysing! What a beast!" The Cardinal spoke out in public sermons and argued the case for firm opposition at bishops conferences. He was also one of the Catholic contacts of the Kreisau Circle of the German Resistance. In 1944, Preysing met with and gave a blessing to Claus von Stauffenberg, in the lead up to the July Plot to assassinate Hitler.

The bishop of Münster, Clemens August Graf von Galen, was Preysing's cousin and another powerful voice of protest against the Nazis. When in 1936 Nazis removed crucifixes in schools, protest by the bishop of Münster led to public demonstration. He denounced the lawlessness of the Gestapo and the cruel program of Nazi euthanasia. He also attacked the Gestapo for seizing church properties and converting them to their own purposes—including use as cinemas and brothels. His three powerful sermons of July and August 1941 earned him the nickname of the "Lion of Münster." The Nazi press called him "enemy number one." Hitler called him a "liar and a traitor," and Goering said he was a "saboteur and agitator."

From the very beginning, Bishop Galen had been just as critical of the National Socialists as he had earlier been of the Weimar Republic. Although initially he opposed National Socialism primarily for ecclesiastical reasons, without questioning the legitimacy of the regime itself, this would change in 1936. In his sermon at the Xanten pilgrimage on September 6, he for the first time formulated something akin to righteous resistance to an unjust regime motivated by human rights and freedom of conscience.

Other fierce opponents of Hitler and his ideology were Bishop Johann Sproll of Rottenberg and Bishop Matthias Ehrenfried of Würzburg. Unfortunately, there were also dissonant voices among the German Catholic leaders. Bishop Conrad Gröber of Freiburg was so compliant to the Third Reich that he was nicknamed the "brown" bishop. And the military Bishop Franz Rarkowski was known for his wartime exhortations.

Then, in March 1937, Pope Pius XI issued the encyclical *Mit Brennender Sorge*—accusing the Nazis of violations of the Concordat, and of sowing the "tares of suspicion, discord, hatred, calumny, of secret and open fundamental hostility to Christ and His Church." The pope noted on the horizon the "threatening storm clouds" of religious wars of extermination over Germany. He also condemned "Whoever exalts race, or the people, or the State, or a particular form of State, or the depositories of power, or any other fundamental value of the human community." No wonder, the Nazis responded with an intensification of the Church suppression. There were mass arrests of clergy and Catholic presses were expropriated. Goebbels renewed the regime's crackdown and propaganda against Catholics. By 1939, all Catholic denominational schools had been disbanded or converted to public facilities.

Subsequent Catholic protests included the March 22, 1942 pastoral letter by the German bishops on "The Struggle against Christianity and the Church." In an effort to counter the strength and influence of spiritual resistance, the security services watched Catholic clergy very closely—instructing that agents monitor every diocese, that the bishops' reports to the Vatican should be obtained, and that bishops' activities be reported. Priests were frequently denounced, arrested, or sent to concentration camps—many to the barracks at Dachau dedicated to clergy. Nazi policy towards the Church was at its most severe in the territories it annexed to Greater Germany, where the Nazis set about systematically dismantling the Church—arresting its leaders, exiling its clergymen, closing its churches, monasteries, and convents. Many clergymen were murdered. Hundreds of priests were arrested for speaking out against the anti-democratic changes and the persecution of Jews. Thousands of members of Germany's Catholic Center Party were in jails or concentration camps, even before the party voted itself out of existence.

More and more bishops voiced their serious concerns. How did they do this? It might be informative to quote more extensively the Bishop of Münster, Clemens August von Galen, who became increasingly outspoken and unambiguous in a 1941 homily:

> We must be prepared that in the near future such terrifying news will accumulate—that even here one religious house after another will be confiscated by the Gestapo and that its occupants, our brothers and sisters, children of our families, loyal German citi-

zens, will be thrown on to the street like outlawed helots and hunted out of the country, like vermin.

Many times, and again quite recently, we have seen the Gestapo arresting blameless and highly respected German men and women without the judgment of any court or any opportunity for defense, depriving them of their freedom, taking them away from their homes interning them somewhere. In recent weeks even two members of my closest council, the chapter of our cathedral, have been suddenly seized from their homes by the Gestapo, removed from Münster and banished to distant places.

Here we are dealing with human beings, with our neighbors, brothers and sisters, the poor and invalids ... unproductive—perhaps! But have they, therefore, lost the right to live? Have you or I the right to exist only because we are 'productive'? ... A curse on men and on the German people if we break the holy commandment: Thou shalt not kill. . . . Woe to us German people if we not only license this heinous offence but allow it to be committed with impunity!

The public protests of the Bishop of Münster did lead to a temporary halt in the killing program. The Nazis were hit and realized they had to take public opinion into account. In the Reich chancellery, some people around Martin Bormann, its head, considered hanging the bishop of Münster to intimidate the other bishops. Hitler wanted him to stand trial before the People's Court. In the end, Joseph Goebbels's position won out. It was decided to postpone dealing with him until the final victory. There was no point, so they reasoned, in creating Catholic martyrs in the middle of a war, which would only drive the Catholic population to the barricades against the Nazi regime.

More and more, the German bishops began to act in unison. In their Pastoral Letter, given on March 22, 1942, they denounced the Nazi euthanasia program and declared their support for human rights, personal freedom under God, and "just laws" of all people:

We demand juridical proof of all sentences and release of all fellow citizens who have been deprived of their liberty without proof. . . . We the German bishops shall not cease to protest against the killing of innocent persons. Nobody's life is safe unless the Commandment, "Thou shalt not kill" is observed. . . . We the bishops, in the name of the Catholic people . . . demand the return of all unlawfully confiscated and in some cases sequestered property . . . for what happens today to church property may tomorrow happen to any lawful property.

How did other countries fare? As early as May 24, 1936 Dutch Roman-Catholic bishops declare that Nazi membership is incompatible with that of the Church. When they voiced even stronger protests, Dutch Catholics took part in strikes and protests against the Nazi treatment of the Jews. Therefore, in July 1942, the Nazis declared that all Jewish converts and Jews married to Gentiles would no longer be exempted from deportation if the opposition ceased. While the Protestant leaders in the Netherlands remained silent, the Dutch Bishops, under leadership of the Archbishop of Utrecht, Johannes de Jong, would not be deterred and on July 26, 1942, issued a decree that openly condemned Nazi deportations of Dutch workers and Jews. The Nazi response was the rounding up of over 40,000 Catholics of Jewish descent, including the future saint Edith Stein, but with the exemption of the 9,000 Protestant Jews. The Pastoral Letter of the Dutch Bishops started as follows:

> We live in a time of great affliction, both spiritual and material. In recent times two specific afflictions have come to the fore: the persecution of the Jews and the unfortunate lot of those who are sent to work in foreign countries. All of us must become fully aware of these troubles, and for this reason, they are now brought to our attention as a community. These afflictions must also be brought to the attention of those who are responsible for them. To this end, the venerable Dutch Episcopate, in communion with nearly all the churches in the Netherlands, approached the authorities of the occupying forces concerning, among other things, the Jews, in a recent telegram of Saturday, July 11. The telegram stated the following: "The undersigned Dutch churches, already deeply shocked by the actions taken against the Jews in the Netherlands that have excluded them from participating in the normal life of society, have learned with horror of the new measures by which men, women, children, and whole families will be deported to the German territory and its dependencies."

A similar story was played out in France and Italy where cardinals, bishops, and priests exhorted the faithful to assist Jews and give them shelter. And when Hitler invaded Hungary in the spring of 1944, the Vatican protested vigorously and regularly against the inhumane treatment of the Jews in Hungary, as did all the Hungarian bishops (including Mindszenty). Catholic churches in Hungary offered conversion to thousands of Jews to save them from prosecution and deportation. Although these actions were done on a local scale, they were also the closest to the Catholics in the pews.

Even if it is true that the conduct of the French, Belgian, Dutch, Polish, and Hungarian bishops in the war years stands in marked contrast to the conduct of their German brethren, one is tempted to conclude that this was due, at least in part, to the different conduct of the French, Belgian, Dutch, Polish, and Hungarian people. Perhaps the German shepherds were more inclined to go along with their flocks, instead of always leading them. Besides, we should never forget that individual Catholics in Germany were dealing with an extremely repressive regime. Any voice of dissent would immediately be silenced. German Catholics were living in an oppressive atmosphere of propaganda, fear of arrest at any moment, and the gnawing worry that everything being said to friends or family might be reported to the Gestapo. Friends, pastors, teachers, and relatives were taken in the night, and only vague and gruesome reports of their deaths or imprisonment followed. Thus many considered it safer to be silent than to be silenced.

Papal Responses

Needing a permanent statement to clarify legally the Catholic Church's status in Nazi Germany, Pius XI signed a concordat with Hitler on July 20, 1933. While attacked today as a Catholic capitulation to the Nazis, the concordat was viewed in its time in terms similar to those of the Concordat of 1800 between Pope Pius VII and Napoleon Bonaparte. In facing a dictator who would surely violate all spoken promises, Pope Pius XI sought a formal document that could be used to defend the rights of Catholics and Catholic institutions in a future Germany that the pontiff knew was going to be dark and dangerous for all who professed faith in Christ.

The Concordat had nothing to do with anti-Semitism; in 1938, Pope Pius XI memorably declared that, in his own words, "anti-Semitism is a movement in which we Christians can have no part whatsoever. . . . Spiritually we are Semites." The future Pope Benedict XVI, who grew up during this horrible time, wrote later that "Even as a child, I could not understand how some people wanted to derive a condemnation of Jews from the death of Jesus. . . . Jesus's blood raises no calls for retaliation but calls all to reconciliation."

In connection with this, we should pay closer attention to the encyclical *Mit Brennender Sorge* (this time written not in Latin but in German) that Pope Pius XI issued on March 1937 (it was co-drafted by Cardinal Faulhaber of Munich, Berlin's Bishop Preysing, Munich's Bishop Galen, and the Vatican Secretary of State Cardinal Pacelli, the future Pope Pius XII). Here are some relevant extracts:

> Whoever identifies, by pantheistic confusion, God and the universe, by either lowering God to the dimensions of the world, or raising the world to the dimensions of God, is not a believer in God. Whoever follows that so-called pre-Christian Germanic conception of substituting a dark and impersonal destiny for the personal God, denies thereby the Wisdom and Providence of God who "Reacheth from end to end mightily, and ordereth all things sweetly" (Wisdom viii:1). Neither is he a believer in God. (Section 7)
>
> Whoever exalts race, or the people, or the State, or a particular form of State, or the depositories of power, or any other fundamental value of the human community—however necessary and honorable be their function in worldly things—whoever raises these notions above their standard value and divinizes them to an idolatrous level, distorts and perverts an order of the world planned and created by God; he is far from the true faith in God and from the concept of life which that faith upholds. (Section 8)
>
> Whoever wishes to see banished from church and school the Biblical history and the wise doctrines of the Old Testament, blasphemes the name of God, blasphemes the Almighty's plan of salvation, and makes limited and narrow human thought the judge of God's designs over the history of the world: he denies his faith in the true Christ. (Section 16)

Catholic priests, nuns, and lay people made it possible for *Mit Brennender Sorge* to be read everywhere. Despite the concerted efforts of the Gestapo, thousands upon thousands of copies were printed through a vast underground network and then distributed through parishes across Nazi Germany. Formal Nazi protests were lodged with the Vatican; Goebbels launched a renewed anti-Catholic propaganda campaign, and the Gestapo arrested hundreds of Catholics, including children who were caught handing out copies of the encyclical. New trials were orchestrated against priests and nuns. A typical Gestapo technique was to lure a priest to a hotel room or apartment on the pretense of someone needing last rites. Once there, the priest was set upon by a prostitute while Gestapo officials took photos of the bewildered victim. The photos were then used at the trial as supposedly damning evidence.

The model for all Catholics during the war itself was the successor of Pius XI, Pope Pius XII, and his heroic and much-documented actions on behalf of Jews in Italy (as we will see below). As the pontiff declared in his 1942 Christmas Message, Catholics should not forget "those hundreds of thousands who, without any fault of their own, sometimes only by reason of their nationality or race, are marked for death or progressive extinction." The Israeli diplomat Pinchas Lapide's 1967 book, *The Last Three Popes and the Jews*, documented that between 700,000 and 860,000 Jews were saved from death by the Church. More might have been done, but Lapide recorded that even as the Polish Catholics were being crushed, Catholic clergy and religious saved at least 15,000 (possibly as many as 50,000) Jews.

Could the pope have intervened more often? On any given occasion, the pontiff had to expect that, in all likelihood, his words would not be heeded. As the war progressed, this unhappy reality was made quite explicit by the Germans. For example, by June of 1942—after numerous appeals had already been made specifically on behalf of Jews—the Vatican Ambassador to Germany, Cesare Orsenigo, reported to Giovanni Baptista Montini, the future Pope Paul VI, who had just lodged yet one more appeal on behalf of a Jewish couple, the following: "I regret that, in addition, I must add that these interventions are not only useless, but they are even badly received." Perhaps the surprising thing, again, is that the Vatican continued to lodge protests anyway in spite of the frustrating conditions.

Could the Pontiffs Pius XI and Pius XII have publicly denounced Hitler's actions more often and more clearly? This question is based on the totally hypothetical assumption that "thousands, perhaps tens of thousands" of additional Jews would perhaps have been saved, if only the two popes had spoken out more often and more clearly. Nobody really knows—it is unknowable. Yet it provides the basis of the charges launched by some against the role of the papacy. First of all, this idea ignores the power and cruelty of the Nazi regime. Second, the idea that public protests by Church leaders might have aroused Europe's Catholic populations to oppose the anti-Jewish measures being carried out by their governments is based on the assumption that whenever a pope or a Catholic bishop says something, Catholics will then automatically fall into line to carry out the Church's "orders." Just think, for a comparison, of the effect of the many strong and repeated statements that the last three Pontiffs and the U.S. Catholic bishops have regularly made against legalized abortion. It is exceedingly naïve to imagine that Catholic Church leaders can simply issue "orders" to their flocks with the expectation that what they say will be carried out; yet it seems to be a common assumption among many who fault Pius XI, and more in particular Pius XII, for not having issued the proper "orders."

On several occasions, Pius XII explained that he was not speaking out because he did not want to make the situation worse. Most historians have tended to dismiss his words in this regard as an unconvincing excuse, but in view of the conditions found in Nazi-occupied Europe for those who lived there, perhaps the pontiff understood better than his critics what the consequences of public challenges to the Nazis by him might have been. If Pius XII did not publicly and specifically condemn the Nazi death camps after learning about them, he also did not publicly and specifically condemn the allied bombing of cities. Though historians of the Holocaust rarely mention it, the killing of the innocent in the latter way is as contrary to Catholic moral teaching as the killing of the innocent in the concentration camps.

Yet the Catholic Church did respond. Was her response exceptional? It was not unique when we realize what Protestant Germany did through its *Bekennende Kirche* (Confessing Church) and through brave men such as Karl Barth, Martin Niemöller, and Dietrich Bonhoeffer. But it does seem exceptional when compared with what the Western world did. When President Franklin D. Roosevelt was asked at a White House press conference in 1930 whether he would recommend a relaxation of immigration restrictions so that Jewish refugees could be received in the country, his reply was, "We have the quota system." The United States did not even boycott the Berlin Olympic Games of 1936, despite the fact that by that time the anti-Semitic Nuremberg Laws had been passed and Jews in Germany were legally deprived of their citizenship.

Then in July 1938, ten days after the invasion of Austria, an international conference was convened in Évian, France at the initiative of President Roosevelt to respond to the plight of the increasing numbers of Jewish refugees fleeing murderous persecution in Europe by the Nazis. The conference was convened for purely political reasons. Roosevelt desired to deflect attention and criticism from his own national policy that severely limited the quota of Jewish refugees admitted to the United States. Not unsurprisingly, none of the 34 participants at the conference took the appeal seriously. As Schoeman remarks, "The only exception were tiny Denmark and Holland. The United States ended up not even filling its miniscule quota of a few thousand European Jews a year" (p. 244).

Could it be that Western countries did not know what was going on in Germany? The facts belie this: the campaigns and intentions of the Third Reich toward the Jews were very well known. As early as April 22, 1933, a *New York Times* correspondent wrote a first-hand description of Dachau. Then on September 6, 1933, the *New York Times* wrote, "Aryanism is now the keystone of Nazi policy.... Its corollary is persecution even to extermination—the word is the Nazis' own—of the non-Aryans." During 1933, several eyewitnesses of the horrors of the concentration camps reported their experiences in the United States and British press, as well as in the British House of Commons. Who could still say "we did not know"?

Five Anti-Catholic Myths

Pius XII and the Jews

Hitler's Pope?

One of the greatest villains in the anti-Catholic myths fabricated around the Holocaust is Pope Pius XII. The nagging question is: how could this man ever have become so controversial?

He certainly was not controversial during the time of World War II and immediately after. Commenting on the pope's 1942 Christmas address, the *New York Times* called the pope "a lonely voice crying out of the silence of a continent." Chaim Weizmann, who would become Israel's first President, wrote in 1943 a letter in which he offered thanks for "the support the Holy See was giving to lend its powerful help whenever it can to mitigate the fate of my coreligionists." Winston Churchill called the pope "the greatest man of our time."

At Pius XII's death on October 9, 1958, he still enjoyed worldwide acclaim. Tributes to the deceased pontiff for his efforts to save Jews during Hitler's Holocaust poured in from all sides. The *New York Times* took three days to print the tributes from New York City rabbis alone. On learning about the pope's death, Israel's Foreign Minister Golda Meir said: "In a generation afflicted by wars and discords, he upheld the highest ideals of peace and compassion." Similar sentiments were expressed by Rome's Chief Rabbi, Israel Zolli, who wrote in his memoir: "There is no place of sorrow where the spirit of love of Pius XII has not reached." One of Zolli's successors, the longtime Chief Rabbi of Rome, Elio Toaff, said at the Pope's death: "More than any other people, the Italian Jews had experienced the great pity and supreme generosity of the Pontiff during the unhappy years of persecution and terror."

And here is a voice from the Nazi camp: The Nazi-Germany newspaper *Morgenpost* of Berlin, on March 3, 1939, greeted the election of Cardinal Pacelli to the papal chair as "not accepted with favor in Germany because he was always opposed to Nazism." Joseph Goebbels had already called this pope "the deputy of the Jew God."

How could the image of Pope Pius XII change so drastically from being a hero to a villain? The turning event came in 1963 in the form (of all things) of a stage play entitled *The Deputy* ("Der Stellvertreter") by the then-32 year old German Rolf Hochhuth. The author, who had been a junior member of the Hitler Youth, portrayed Pope Pius XII as a cold-hearted cynic, more interested in the Vatican's investment portfolio than in Hitler's slaughter of the Jews. Yet for all of its inaccuracies and even crudities, *The Deputy* was a huge success and, virtually by itself, launched a Pius XII controversy. The pope's reputation flipped so quickly and completely—without any new evidence being disclosed—that something else must have been going on. A first indication of a wider plot was the fact that the play was translated into more than twenty languages by translators who all happened to be Western communists or sympathizers. In what can only be described as a cruel twist of events, the pope—who had been widely celebrated for his wartime leadership—suddenly came under fire and was denounced for his alleged silence and indifference.

The play caricatured and vilified Pius XII just as Communist propagandists used to condemn their enemies. Indeed, there is a proven connection between the two. As early as the winter of 1944–45, shortly before the end of the Second World War, the Soviet newspaper *Pravda* called the pope a fascist and an ally of Hitler. At the end of World War II, the Soviet Union continued an aggressive campaign to defame Pius XII. Then, almost twenty years later, Hochhuth intensified this anti-Pius propaganda. In the summer of 1963, the Vatican pointed out "numerous similarities" between Hochhuth's play and "the usual communist propaganda against the Church and the Pope"—among them the charge of a "common crusade with Hitler against the Soviet Union." Interestingly enough, the first producer of the play, Erwin Piscator, had joined the German Communist Party in 1919 and worked for Soviet intelligence in Moscow during World War II. Without Piscator, the play that framed Pius XII would most likely never have seen the light of day.

We now know for sure that the Soviets assigned agents to concoct lies about the Church, depicting Pius XII as being silent about the Holocaust, as pro-Nazi, and indeed "Hitler's Pope." Most recently, General Ion Pacepa, a former high-level official in Romania's Communist dictatorship of Ceausescu and the highest-ranking official ever to defect from the Soviet Union, has given us details about the

Soviet plot to defame Pius XII. In KGB jargon, changing pasts was called "framing" and constituted a highly classified "disinformation" specialty. The framing of Pope Pius XII began on June 3, 1945, when Radio Moscow mendaciously alleged that he was "Hitler's Pope." Pacepa has recently revealed that he himself played an important role in this "disinformation" machinery, and that he had sent Romanian agents to the Vatican disguised as priests. They gained access to the archives and copied documents which, carefully falsified, were made available to Hochhuth, who was then conducting research in Rome.

It was an attempt to shift the guilt from "the many" in the West and lay it on the shoulders of "one man" in the Vatican. Not many seemed to realize that the playwright himself is by no means a friend of the Jews. All Jews who appear in the play are caricatures and freaks; not one of them is an upright man. Nevertheless, for more than forty years, the pope's "silence" has supplied headlines for the media—without the same media ever questioning Hochhuth's silence, even though he still refuses to identify his Vatican contacts. In 1969, Rabbi Marc Tanenbaum challenged fellow Jews to resist endorsing Hochhuth's allegations and being manipulated and exploited by opportunists who did not have their best interests at heart.

So persistent was the controversy in the 1960s that Pope Paul VI, who as Archbishop G.B. Montini had been one of Pius XII's principal assistants during the war years, waived the strict time limits of 45 years governing access to the archives of the Vatican Secretariat of State; he assigned three Jesuit historians to search the archives and prepare for publication all the documents pertaining to the Vatican's activity during the war. The idea was to provide solid documentation for the role of Pius XII and the Vatican during that conflict. The results of the intense labors of these scholars, completed in 1981, amounted to twelve volumes published under the title "Acts and Documents of the Holy See relative to the Second World War" (abbreviated as ADSS).

However, Paul VI's hope that opening up the documents might help resolve the controversy did not really settle anything. The voices for and against Pius XII just became louder and louder. Rabbi David G. Dalin was right when he noted in *The Weekly Stan-*

dard of February 26, 2001 that some of the bitterest attacks on Pius XII have been made by disaffected Catholics; as he put it, this "disparages the testimony of Holocaust survivors and thins out, by spreading to inappropriate figures, the condemnation that belongs to Hitler and the Nazis."

Here are some offenses Pope Pius XII has been accused of committing since the infamous play of Hochhuth:

Mock offense #1: Pius XII made a pact with Hitler

The facts belie this. Eugenio Pacelli (the pope's original name) was sent to Germany as nuncio in the free state of Bavaria in 1917, and then to Prussia in 1925. During this time, the man who had worked on the systemization of canon law in the 1917 Code—meant as a crucial step toward securing the Church's sovereignty—wanted to make sure the Church would continue to keep her sovereignty. Without concordats the internal life of the Church would remain vulnerable to secular domination and control. Therefore, while in Germany, he negotiated a favorable concordat between the Holy See and Bavaria in 1924, and a less favorable one with Prussia in 1929. A concordat may be hard to understand for citizens of the United States, given their Constitution, but in a European context, where the state has many more powers, it is a treaty that guarantees liberty for the Church to manage its own affairs without state supervision or interference.

When Hitler grabbed dictatorial power in 1933, making a concordat with the new government became an urgent necessity for the Church, who was clearly concerned to protect the rights of Catholics in Nazi Germany. This is why Pope Pius XI signed a "contract" (concordat) with Hitler. Interestingly enough, the initiative for the treaty did not come from the Vatican this time, but from Hitler, who wanted to remove Catholic clergymen from party politics. Franz von Papen, a Nazi in Catholic garb, was sent to Rome to conclude this pact, but received a cool reception from the then-Secretary of State Pacelli, who was fully aware of how little faith could be placed in Hitler's promises.

When a new negotiator was sent to Rome, Pacelli continued to refuse agreement to the withdrawal of clergy from political activity, until it became clear that the Catholic Center Party in Germany was about to dissolve itself as the last German party to hold out against Hitler. Then things moved quickly. The concordat was initialed in Rome on July 8, 1933. It was a "pact" meant to protect Catholics in Germany, but certainly not Hitler.

Mock offense #2: Pius XII did not speak out against Hitler

The facts of the matter are these. While still Secretary of State, Pacelli took the lead in drafting the encyclical *Mit Brennender Sorge*, issued by Pope Pius XI in March of 1937. It was an encyclical written in German (in a change from the traditional Latin) to make sure it would "reach" Germany. The document excoriated the Nazis for repeated violations of the concordat and contained a clear rejection of the Nazi doctrine of racial purity:

> Whoever exalts race, or the people, or the State, or a particular form of State, or the depositories of power, or any other funda-mental value of the human community—however necessary and honorable be their function in worldly things—whoever raises these notions above their standard value and divinizes them to an idolatrous level, distorts and perverts an order of the world planned and created by God; he is far from the true faith in God and from the concept of life which that faith upholds.

During his time as Vatican Secretary of State, Pacelli frequently spoke out against the Nazis, including one notable speech in 1935 to 250,000 people at Lourdes when he said that the Nazis

> are in reality only miserable plagiarists who dress up old errors with new tinsel. It does not make any difference whether they flock to the banners of social revolution, whether they are guided by a false concept of the world and of life, or whether they are pos-sessed by the superstition of a race and blood cult.

Following the death of Pius XI on February 10, 1939, Pacelli suc-ceeded him as pontiff. His first encyclical, *Summi Pontificatus*, was issued on October 20, 1939, less than two months after Hitler's inva-sion of Poland. Heinrich Müller, head of the Gestapo in Berlin, wrote that the encyclical was "directed exclusively against Germany, both in ideology and in regard to the German-Polish dispute."

Müller read the encyclical correctly:

> Once the authority of God and the sway of His law are denied in this way, the civil authority as an inevitable result tends to attribute to itself that absolute autonomy which belongs exclusively to the Supreme Maker. It puts itself in the place of the Almighty and elevates the State or group into the last end of life, the supreme criterion of the moral and juridical order, and therefore forbids every appeal to the principles of natural reason and of the Christian conscience.... To consider the State as something ultimate to which everything else should be subordinated and directed, cannot fail to harm the true and lasting prosperity of nations.... What used to appear on the outside as order, was nothing but an invasion of disorder: confusion in the principles of moral life.... The blood of countless human beings, even noncombatants, raises a piteous dirge over a nation such as Our dear Poland.

Between 2003 and 2006, the archives of the pontificate of Pius XII's predecessor, Pius XI, were released, demonstrating that his Secretary of State, Pacelli, fiercely opposed Nazi doctrine and practices, and supported the Third Reich's many victims. Pacelli may have acquired a lifelong admiration for German discipline and order while being a nuncio in Germany, but he certainly had not become a Nazi ally—quite the opposite. But it cannot be denied that Pacelli had been trained in Church diplomacy, which is focused on the interests of the Church, sometimes more than the truth of the Gospel. The worst that can be said about him in this respect, as some have done, is that he used "a diplomatic remedy for a moral outrage."

The fact remains, though, that Pius XII did speak out against Hitler on many occasions. Could he have spoken more and thus saved more people? Such a question is a matter of speculation; history does not tell us the answer. Ironically, scholars of history can go on, year after year, producing volumes targeting the Pope for what did *not* happen in history. And besides, when focusing exclusively on one issue—the Pope and the Jews—one might lose sight of the fact that there was a *war* going on. The 107-odd acres of Vatican City were entirely surrounded by a hostile Fascist regime in Italy, which, not incidentally, also controlled the Vatican's water, electricity, food supply, mail delivery, garbage removal, and, indeed, the very physical accessibility by anybody from outside Vatican City. Moreover, the resistance of the Dutch bishops, for instance, shows us that "speaking out" did not always save lives but sometimes actually cost them.

Mock offense #3: Pius XII was Hitler's Pope

After all that has been said, this rebuttal can be short. John Cornwell's notorious 1999 book *Hitler's Pope* suggests that Pacelli, the pope-to-be, had visited Hitler. In fact, Pacelli never set foot on Nazi soil after he left Germany for good in 1929—which is four years before Hitler obtained power. Furthermore, Pius XII never even met Hitler, much less collaborated with him. The two were implacable opponents. The photograph on the front cover of the American edition of Cornwell's book had been manipulated in order to give the impression that Pius had just visited Hitler in March 1939, the month that Pacelli was made Pope, when, in fact, the photo had been taken in 1927, before Hitler had taken over, as Pius was leaving a reception held for German President Paul von Hindenburg.

Not only did Pius XII speak out against the Holocaust, he was one of the first ones to do so, authorizing Vatican Radio to explicitly condemn Nazi atrocities against Jews and Catholics in Poland, and personally confronting German Foreign Minister Joachim Ribbentrop over them. Robert Kempner, a prosecutor at the post-war Nuremberg Tribunal, publicly praised Pius XII for issuing countless protests against German war crimes. Moreover, the pope's secular power—as ruler of fewer than a thousand inhabitants of Vatican City—is negligible, but depends "upon the spiritual sovereignty of the Holy See" which is indeed *sui generis* and wields an enormous, though imponderable spiritual authority. The matter is succinctly summed up in Stalin's remark, "How many divisions has the pope?" and in Churchill's answer, "A number of legions not always visible on parade."

John Cornwell's book *Hitler's Pope* had certainly the wrong title; it should have been called *Hitler's Sworn Enemy*, instead, especially when one considers the Pope's close contacts with the anti-Nazi resistance and his approval of a plot to overthrow Hitler. Kenneth L. Woodward in *Newsweek* magazine for September 27, 1999, noted about Cornwell's book that "errors of fact and ignorance of context appear on almost every page." Authors like Cornwell—and many others unfortunately—begin their books with pre-conceived ideas against Pius XII, and then write their books to shape those theories.

Of all the books that are still being published on Pope Pius XII, some are pro-Pius, some are anti-Pius—there seems to be hardly any that fall in between the extremes. Given the still existing anti-Pius bias, it is not surprising that the anti-Pius books have a much better chance to make it to the best-seller lists. Kenneth D. Whitehead (a former career diplomat who served in Rome and the Middle East and as the chief of the Arabic Service of the Voice of America) reviewed several of them and came to the following conclusion:

> These anti-Pius books too are the ones published by mainstream New York publishers such as Doubleday and Knopf or by university presses, and they are also the ones most likely to be found on public library or bookstore shelves. All four of the pro-Pius books, by contrast, are published by small religious publishers with much less access to bookstore sales and a wide readership. Nor do the pro-Pius books appear to have been reviewed either as widely or as often as the anti-Pius ones; so it seems to be a simple fact that the latter have largely shaped the debate to date. Even so . . . I think the pro-Pius books still have much the better of the argument.

Unfortunately, too many people are still stuck in the did-he-or-did-he-not questions that have characterized the Pius XII controversy—instead of asking the question as to why this heroic good man is being defamed. In a controversy like this, favorable evidence tends to be read in the worst light and treated to the strictest test, while unfavorable evidence is read in the best light.

The Pope's Jews

Correcting the image from "Hitler's Pope" to "The Pope's Jews" has not been an easy process. An event that has been colored the most by the pope's distorted image took place on October 16, 1943—famously called "Black Saturday." In the early hours of that day, during the German occupation of Rome, Nazi troops descended upon Rome's Jews, estimated to be at last 8,000. The intent, following order from Berlin, was to seize and deport all of them.

An Italian princess, Enza Pignatelli Aragona, was one of the first to witness the victims being loaded in trucks early in the morning of October 16, 1943. She hastened to the Vatican, where she was known, and was admitted to the pope's private apartment, where she conveyed the news of the round-up to him. An obviously agitated pope exclaimed that he had been "promised" that the Roman Jews would not be touched. In her presence, the pontiff immediately made a telephone call—it is unknown to whom, although some believe it was to his Secretary of State, Cardinal Luigi Maglione, to instruct him to lodge an immediate protest with the German Ambassador. Cardinal Maglione did, in fact, meet with Ambassador von Weizsäcker that day and asked him to intervene "in favor of these poor people." Weizsäcker's role in the affair has often been disputed, especially since this German envoy is supposed to have feared that Hitler might take rash action against the Vatican if provoked; and hence his reports to Berlin were apparently often couched in language aimed at keeping Hitler calm on the subject of the Vatican.

What happened that day—and what Pope Pius XII's role was in its harrowing events—has been debated and written about for decades. The event has been immortalized in the well-known movie *The Scarlet and the Black*. Unfortunately, the movie creates the impression that Monsignor Hugh O'Flaherty, the main player in the movie and the legendary Irish member of the Curia, acted on his own, without any guidance from Pope Pius XII. Writings of and memories about the Monsignor have revealed that he was acting on the orders of Pius XII. So it wasn't he who first created the rescue network; it wasn't he who set up safe houses for Allied soldiers and Jews; it wasn't he who sent the food trucks out to feed them—it was the pope, whom Monsignor O'Flaherty loyally, wholeheartedly, and enthusiastically served.

The same can be said about another underground network, portrayed in the movie *The Assisi Underground*. In September 1943, Fra Ruffino Niccacci was the Guardian of the Franciscan Monastery of

San Damiano in Assisi. At the direction of Bishop Placido Nicolini and Aldo Brunacci, secretary to the bishop and chairman of the Committee to Aid Refugees, Padre Ruffino provided Jews with false identities and gave them sanctuary in monasteries and convents. Again, the orders to do so came ultimately from the Vatican. The Jewish historian Anna Foa has made this very clear in more general terms:

> the ways in which the work of sheltering and rescuing the persecuted was carried forward were such that they could not have been simply the fruit of initiatives from below, but were clearly coordinated as well as permitted by the leadership of the Church. This erases the image proposed in the 1960s of a Pope Pius XII indifferent to the fate of the Jews or even an accomplice of the Nazis.

The pope's leadership in all these efforts was not limited to Italy. A special mention should be made of the many papal nuncios who, under the direction of Pius XII, tirelessly worked to assist the persecuted in the countries they were assigned to. Exceptional in this regard were the nuncios Andrea Cassulo in Romania, Angelo Rotta in Hungary, Angelo Roncalli, the future John XXII, in Greece and Turkey, and Giovanni Ferrofino in Haiti.

Although the ruthless Nazis were able to round up more than 1,200 Jews during Black Saturday, and would deport more than 1,000 of these to the Auschwitz-Birkenau extermination camp in Poland, the vast majority of them—over 85%—survived. They were being hidden and protected in Church-run institutions with Pius XII's knowledge and support. The pope even opened up his own summer residence at Castel Gandolfo to take in Jews targeted for death. As the U.S. Holocaust Memorial Museum notes: "For every Jew caught by the Germans in Rome, at least ten escaped and hid, many in the Vatican." Numerous people urged Pius XII to flee—and a lesser man would have done so—but instead Pius XII remained solidly at his post in Rome, leading the Church, but also the anti-Nazi resistance. It must be mentioned, though, that Pius XII did prepare a letter of resignation, so that, if he were captured by the Nazis, he would no longer be the pope, but an ex-pope, a simple cardinal, not the Head of the Church.

How real was the fear for the safety of the pope? From September of 1943 to June of 1944, Rome was under harsh German military occupation, and it was during this period that Hitler seriously considered occupying the Vatican and abducting Pius XII. Given the Vatican's experience, this was not an imaginary threat at all: both the French Revolution and Napoleon had done precisely that in the cases of Pius VI and Pius VII, having abducted both popes by military force and transported them beyond the Alps (Pius VI died in exile in France). As to Pius XII, there were obviously troubling precedents for what Hitler was reported to be considering—and such reports did come to him. Before June 4, 1944, when the Allies liberated Rome, there was never a time that Pius XII and his Vatican colleagues did not have to fear a possible Vatican takeover by armed force.

How has all this information changed the view we have of Pope Pius XII? Let us find out the impact it has had on Israel's World Holocaust Center, *Yad Vashem*. The Center was established in 1953 in the hope that Jews and the world would know everything that could be known about the Holocaust. It has two main sections: a Hall of Remembrance where the victims and their enormous sufferings are presented, and the Memorial's Museum where judgments and claims are made about what had happened. It is in the second section that visitors may get the impression that the Museum still promotes a distorted image of Pope Pius XII. The original 2005 text on Pius XII still echoes the anti-papal propaganda of Hochhuth's play.

The Museum distinguishes three categories of people among the Gentiles: the perpetrators, the righteous, and the silent bystanders. The pontiff ended up in the third category as not being a righteous person who risked his life to save others—but being guilty, not of the commission of evil but of the omission of good. Although nominated in the past, Pius XII has been routinely rejected for the honor of Righteous Gentile. Although plenty of evidence exists for his efforts to save Jews, the main obstacle for honoring him is probably that this would also honor the Catholic Church, which is seen by many as a complicit in, and not a victim of, the Holocaust. However, this leaves us wondering if what the Museum staff does to the

Catholic Church is not similar to what anti-Semites do to Jews. At least the general role of protection that the Church played toward the Jews in Italy has been acknowledged: Cardinal Dalla Costa of Florence, Fr. Francesco Repetto of Genoa, Cardinal Chuster of Milan, and Fra Ruffino Niccacci of Assisi all have been proclaimed Righteous. So should Pius XII be next?

In 2007, the text about Pius XII was revised, and it at least acknowledged that Pius XII condemned racial mass murder in his 1942 Christmas message. Further, we are told that "the Pontiff offered encouragement to activities in which Jews were rescued." But the text still asserts that he suppressed statements from his predecessor drafted against racism and anti-Semitism, titled "On the Unity of the Human Race"—whereas in fact, Pius XII took the best parts of those drafts and inserted them into his own first encyclical, *Summi Pontificatus*, subtitled "On the Unity of Human Society." In a reaction to the text change of the Holocaust Museum, Sir Martin Gilbert, a leading Jewish historian of the modern world at Oxford University, called the 2007 text "distorted shorthand."

In 2012, another revision was made after bringing together a group of historians to reassess Pius XII's legacy based on the latest research. The new text does indeed further acknowledge the Vatican's role in the protection and rescue of Jews. *Yad Vashem* also stated that it is open to additional changes and revisions, but not until the Vatican releases the remaining archives of Pius XII's pontificate (which Pope Francis may do shortly). The tide seems to be changing. But it must also be stated that some commentators constantly contradict themselves—urging everyone to withhold judgment on Pius XII until all the Vatican's wartime archives are released, while simultaneously issuing hostile comments which categorically denounce Pius XII. Besides, the publication of the twelve volumes of actual Vatican wartime documents in the ADSS collection does not have brought the question any closer to settlement, so the opening to scholars of the rest of the Vatican archives for the period is likely to fail as well.

I hope I have made clear why the image of Pope Pius XII has changed so radically from being a hero to a villain. But we still need to wait for the general tide to turn back again. This proves how tenacious myths can be. Could it be that the same power which gave Hitler extraordinary powers is also the source behind the tenacity of these anti-Catholic myths? If so, we have a fierce enemy to combat.

Conclusion

D id the Catholic Church make mistakes when it comes to slavery, crusades, inquisitions, Galileo, and the Holocaust? She certainly did:

• All too often she followed the morals of society instead of questioning them from a religious perspective (slavery).

• All too often she let her ideals be overgrown by greed and prejudice (crusades).

• All too often she let her battle against heresy be tainted with inhuman procedures and pressure (inquisitions).

• All too often she was authoritarian, narrow-minded, and hampered by contemporary opinions (Galileo).

• All too often she was more concerned about the interests of the Church than about the common interests of humanity (Holocaust).

Should the Church be blamed for those failures? Of course, she should, but we need to see her failures in the proper context:

• The Church is made up of human beings who are sinners. To paraphrase G.K. Chesterton, as far as sin is concerned, there are two kinds of people: not, as you might think, those who sin and those who do not sin, but those who know they are sinners and those who do not know they are sinners.

• Not only are her members human, but the Church as an institution can also fail. Unless the Church proclaims a matter of doctrine ex cathedra, she is fallible.

• The Church's social teaching is based on unchanging principles, but the circumstances that they apply to constantly change.

• Even when the Church officially proclaims her social teaching, her members may not automatically fall into line to carry out the

Church's "orders." Every pope knows all too well that there is no instant obedience of his Church members at a mere snap of his fingers. We cannot blame the Church for this.

• The Church is an extension of the Incarnation, the Body of the one Christ. Like Christ, she has a divine nature and a human nature. Unlike Christ, her human nature is far from perfect.

• In spite of errors made in dealing with slavery, the crusades, the inquisition, the Galileo case, and the Holocaust, we should remember the words of Cardinal John Henry Newman: "One vessel alone can ride those waves; it is the boat of Peter, the ark of God." This is the ark that cannot sink till the end of time.

• It is the papacy alone that has the divine promise of time.

I could not summarize this better than quoting what Pope Benedict XVI said during his 2007 visit to Austria: "God can write straight even on the crooked lines of our history."

Suggested Reading

Hannam, James. *God's Philosophers: How the Medieval World Laid the Foundations of Modern Science.* London: Icon Books, 2009.

Jaki, Stanley L. *The Savior of Science.* Grand Rapids, MI: Eerdmans, 2000.

Kamen, Henry. *The Spanish Inquisition: A Historical Revision.* New Haven, CT: Yale University Press, 1999.

Kilpatrick, William. *Christianity, Islam, and Atheism: The Struggle for the Soul of the West.* San Francisco, CA: Ignatius Press, 2012.

Lapide, Pinchas. *The Last Three Popes and the Jews.* London: Souvenir Press, 1967.

Madden Thomas F. *A Concise History of the Crusades.* Lanham, MD: Rowman & Littlefield, 2005.

McInerny, Ralph. *The Defamation of Pius XII.* South Bend, IN: St. Augustine's Press, 2001.

Panzer, Joel. *The Popes and Slavery.* Staten Island, NY: Alba House, 1996.

Peters, Edward. *Inquisition.* Berkeley, CA: University of California Press, 1988.

Rychlak, Ronald J. *Hitler, the War, and the Pope.* Huntington, IN: Our Sunday Visitor, 2010.

Schoeman, Roy. *Salvation Is from the Jews.* San Francisco, CA: Ignatius Press, 2003.

Shea, William R. and Artigas, Mariano. *Galileo in Rome: The Rise and Fall of a Troublesome Genius.* Oxford University Press, USA, 2004.

Thomas, Gordon. *The Pope's Jews: The Vatican's Secret Plan to Save Jews from the Nazis.* New York, NY: St. Martin's Press, 2012.

Ventresca, Robert A. *Soldier of Christ: The Life of Pius XII.* Cambridge, MA: Harvard University Press, 2013.

Index

About the Author

Gerard M. Verschuuren is a human geneticist who also earned a doctorate in the philosophy of science. He studied and worked at universities in Europe and the United States. Currently, he is semi-retired and spends most of his time as a writer, speaker, and consultant on the interface of science and religion, creation and evolution, faith and reason.

His most recent books are:

Darwin's Philosophical Legacy—The Good and the Not-So-Good (Lanham, MD: Lexington Books, 2012).

God and Evolution?—Science Meets Faith (Boston, MA: Pauline Books, 2012).

Of All That Is, Seen and Unseen—Life-Saving Answers to Life-Size Questions (Goleta, CA: Queenship Publishing, 2012).

What Makes You Tick?—A New Paradigm for Neuroscience (Antioch, CA: Solas Press, 2012).

The Destiny of the Universe—In Pursuit of the Great Unknown (St. Paul, MN: Paragon House, 2014).

It's All in the Genes!—Really? (Amazon, 2014)

Life's Journey—A Guide from Conception to Natural Death (Kettering, OH: Angelico Press, forthcoming, 2015).

For more info see: http://en.wikipedia.org/wiki/Gerard_Verschuuren
He can be contacted at www.where-do-we-come-from.com

www.ingramcontent.com/pod-product-compliance
Lightning Source LLC
Chambersburg PA
CBHW022008080426
42733CB00007B/520